TT™ Titans

The Twenty-five Greatest
Isle of Man Racing Machines

Matthew Richardson

PEN & SWORD
TRANSPORT

First published in Great Britain in 2018 by
Pen & Sword Transport
an imprint of
Pen & Sword Books Ltd
47 Church Street
Barnsley
South Yorkshire
S70 2AS

ISBN 978 1 52671 021 5

A CIP catalogue record for this book is available from the British Library

Typeset in 11/14 & Sabon LT Std
Typeset by Aura Technology and Software Services, India
Printed and bound in India by Replika Press Pvt. Ltd.

Pen & Sword Books Ltd incorporates the imprints of Pen & Sword Archaeology,
Atlas, Aviation, Battleground, Discovery, Family History, History, Maritime,
Military, Naval, Politics, Railways, Select, Social History, Transport, True Crime, and
Claymore Press, Frontline Books, Leo Cooper, Praetorian Press, Remember When,
Seaforth Publishing and Wharncliffe.

For a complete list of Pen & Sword titles please contact
PEN & SWORD BOOKS LIMITED
47 Church Street, Barnsley, South Yorkshire, S70 2AS, England
E-mail: enquiries@pen-and-sword.co.uk
Website: www.pen-and-sword.co.uk

Contents

Acknowledgments

I would be the first to admit that although I have a great deal of interest in the Isle of Man TT and its history, I am by no means an expert. In preparing this book, however, this was less of a handicap than it might have been. I was able to draw on the expertise of many people with a far greater level of knowledge than my own, who advised me on both technical matters and historical points.

In no particular order, I would like to thank them all warmly for their assistance. Firstly I must mention Bill Snelling and his TT Race Pics website. Bill provided a number of the photographs for the book, and also a good deal of sage advice. He was also kind enough to read the book in draft form and offered his comments and corrections. Similarly, John Ridout was kind enough to look through the text and offered important amendments. Dave Collister pointed me towards a number of photographs from his amazing collection, and for these I am also grateful. More examples of Dave's work can be found in his two *Shutterspeed* books, and his calendars are also a marvellous showcase for his work.

Ivan Rhodes provided a great deal of information and assistance regarding the Stanley Woods Velocette, and I stand in awe of his knowledge of the marque, accumulated over a lifetime of study. I also owe a great deal to Dave Molyneux, whose encyclopaedic knowledge of sidecar racing is rivalled only by his skill as a driver. I worked with Dave on his autobiography *The Racer's Edge*, still widely regarded as one of the most insightful TT or racing memoirs. It was Dave's passion for the history of the event and the machines that win it that sparked my own interest in the subject. TT collector Elwyn Roberts was also generous with his knowledge, and I thank him warmly. Helen Gibson was kind enough to offer advice and suggestions. Through the help of Sharon Bowness, the late and sadly missed John Surtees provided me with information relevant to Chapter 8. It must have been one of the last of many acts of kindness, as he passed away just a few weeks later. I remain extremely grateful for his assistance. Jeff Ray at the Barber Motorsports Museum also provided information for Chapter 8, and I thank him for it.

Jack Muldoon, friend of the late, great Jock Taylor, offered me invaluable insights into the history of Jock's quadruple TT-winning sidecar outfit from the early 1980s. In this regard I am also enormously grateful to Bengt-Goran ('Benga') Johansson, Jock's former passenger, who also read and advised me on this chapter. Mick Grant provided a great deal of help and advice regarding his 1978 machine, as did Kenny Arthur in relation to the 1977 O'Dell sidecar outfit. I thank them all most sincerely. The chapter covering Mike Hailwood's Ducati is heavily based on material made available to me by Steve Wynne, and I am indebted to him both for this and for the advice which he gave having read the draft text. I am tremendously grateful to Ken Sprayson, who generously allowed me to use his fantastic colour photographs. Ted Macauley kindly allowed me to quote from his book *Mike the Bike Again*, and also offered his encouragement and support. From the German sidecar racing fraternity, Ulrich Schmidt and Dieter Busch offered advice for which I am enormously grateful. The Isle of Man TT Press Office, and in particular Simon Crellin, were extremely supportive and supplied a number of the illustrations that appear here.

Manx National Heritage supplied a number of illustrations, and for her help in this area I thank my colleague Wendy Thirkettle. Andrew Dawrant at the Royal Aero Club archive kindly supplied a photo of Oliver Godfrey. My friend and former colleague John Caley once again excelled himself in helping me to prepare images for publication, and once again the quality of his work testifies to his enormous skill as a graphic designer. For more information about his work, visit his website johncaleyillustration.com.

Finally, it goes without saying that any errors or omissions which occur in the text are entirely my own responsibility.

Introduction

It was while idling away a few spare hours in my garden that this book began to take shape. I began to imagine what the line-up in a fantasy TT museum would look like. For those who are unfamiliar with it, the Isle of Man TT is the most challenging motorcycle race on earth. Its 37¾-mile track twists through villages and between stone walls and telegraph poles, before climbing over 1,000 feet above sea level to reach the highest point on the course. It tests rider and machine to the limit. There is little margin for error, and for this reason the event has sometimes caused controversy. It is, however, arguably the most historic motorsport event in the world, with the TT Mountain Course being the oldest motorcycle racing circuit on the planet still in use. Only the two world wars, and the threat of foot and mouth disease in 2001, have interrupted the annual event.

The TT is unique: in order to succeed, a rider must display an extraordinary combination of skill and raw courage, coupled with engineering and technical excellence. In this book I examine twenty-five of the most significant machines in the history of the event, combined with profiles of the men who built and rode them. I freely acknowledge that other similar compilations have appeared in the past, but in most cases authors have chosen to focus on significant *types* of machine. What I believe makes this book slightly different, is that I have tried to identify the twenty-five *individual* machines which I believe have made the strongest contribution to TT history. Choosing which to include was a highly subjective process. Perhaps none of the bikes featured in this book would have been successful, had they not been in the hands of the person who took them across the start line that day (it is, after all, a racing truism that the most important component of a motorcycle is the nut holding the handlebars). I admit that another author might well choose a different twenty-five, which would still be equally valid. One of the great things about the TT is that almost every year history is made in some way, so even if this list were definitive, it could not long remain so.

TT fans today might question the inclusion of so many early machines, when more recent lap times and speeds would seem to put them decisively in the shade. However, it is important to remember that pre-1945 riders had fewer races each year from which to build an impressive tally of wins, and the standards of both machinery and road surfaces were much worse. Poor brakes and dusty unmade road surfaces contributed to many accidents in the early years of the event, and I would argue that these early pioneers with pudding basin helmets were no less skillful or brave than their later counterparts.

In selecting the machines, I have tried to weigh up the impact that each had at the time, and in particular I have taken account of achievements such as lap records broken or other significant milestones established. I'm privileged to have seen at least some of the motorbikes and sidecar outfits featured in this book at close hand; I've looked upon them with awe, and I'm gratified to think that at least some of them are preserved for ever as a testament to the skill and bravery of those who built and rode them. While some of the motorcycles I have described are preserved in private or public collections, others are believed to have been lost to history, though it is difficult to be absolutely definitive. Some machines I know still exist; others I know certainly do not. Some I'm still not sure about, so if you know anything about the fate of these machines, why not drop me a line? I can be contacted through the publishers, or I'm usually to be found at the Manx Museum in Douglas.

Matthew Richardson, Douglas, Isle of Man 2017

Chapter 1

432cc Matchless (rider Charlie Collier) 1907

It almost goes without saying that the motorbike that won the first ever Isle of Man TT race, which was held on the St John's course in 1907, would have to be in anyone's collection of the top twenty-five TT machines. But which bike did win that first event? There were two races run as one that year. In the twin-cylinder class, the Norton of Rem Fowler (from Birmingham, and a skilled toolmaker by trade) was the first machine home. In the single-cylinder class Charlie Collier, aboard a Matchless, took the honours. In essence, this chapter is the story of two rival machines and their riders. While Fowler's moment of glory was brief, Collier, it might be argued, has a more lasting claim to fame, not just because he was riding a machine he had built himself, but also because he could justifiably state that he was one of the men who founded the TT itself. Thus it is the Matchless that takes the limelight as the first of the twenty-five greatest-ever Isle of Man racing machines.

Most general history books list Rem Fowler as the first winner of a TT, but it is hard to see why this should be so, because even allowing for the fact that the first-ever race comprised two classes, Collier both won his class *and* finished first overall. Comparison of the two winning machines makes for interesting reading. There was a slight difference in weight, with the twin at 182lb and the single at 171lb, but this was offset by the fact that the former was rated at 5 horsepower and the latter only 3.5 horsepower. Fowler was aboard a Peugeot-engined Norton, the Birmingham-based brand not yet having devised a motor of its own, while Collier was aboard a Matchless, the marque which he, his father Henry and his older brother Harry had developed themselves at their Plumstead works. Like Norton, they had yet to perfect their own powerplant. Along with many other motorcycle manufacturers of the time, they had initially started production as a bicycle-making factory, before deciding to add an engine to their standard frame. In 1905, they produced a JAP V-twin-powered bike, with one of the earliest swing-arm rear suspensions, coupled with leading-link front forks, and they would still be using a 432cc overhead valve JAP engine (along with a belt drive and bicycle-style stirrup brakes) in 1907. Founder John Alfred Prestwich started the JAP engine company in 1895 and, as well as constructing his own motorcycles, he supplied engines to many other manufacturers. They had a well-deserved reputation for strength and reliability.

Over the preceding few years, Harry and Charlie Collier had been racing motorcycles made in their south London factory at events up and down England. They also raced on the Continent, and it was on a train journey back from the 1906 International Cup Races in Austria that the Collier brothers, together with their travel companions, the Marquis de Mouzilly St Mars and Freddie Straight, chairman of the Auto Cycle Club (the motorcycle branch of the Automobile Club), came up with the idea of establishing a two-wheeled race on the Isle of Man. Even at this early point in motorcycle sport, international politics had an influence. By racing closer to home, the Colliers hoped to overcome what they saw as the unfair advantages that European manufacturers enjoyed on the Continent. Collier remembered later:

> Due to the glaring breaches of the rules on the part of the Austrian riders and officials alike, the results of the 1906 race were declared void. Although the continental riders were really splendid fellows it was perfectly obvious that their conception of playing the game was very different from the English version... It was during the long monotonous train journey that the question of organising an English race was discussed and that splendid sportsman, the Marquis de Mouzilly St Mars... generously offered to present a suitable trophy which he suggested should be named the Tourist Trophy.[1]

The Collier family also wanted to see an end to the use of special machines constructed only for racing, and instead wanted to restrict the meeting purely to road-going motorcycles, as a means of testing both reliability and fuel consumption. The Isle of Man was the obvious place to consider holding such an event because, while the Westminster parliament had set its face against closing roads for racing, its smaller cousin on the Island had already established a precedent by closing roads for motorcar racing as early as 1904, and so the Manx authorities were approached. The result of these efforts was the first Tourist Trophy motorcycle race, held on 28 May 1907. Single-cylinder machines were required to achieve a fuel consumption figure of 90mpg; for twin-cylinder machines the target was set at 75mpg. Petrol tanks were specified to be 1.25 gallons in capacity, tyres were required to be of at least

2-inch section, and there was to be a compulsory ten-minute stop for rest and refuelling halfway through the race.

The day of that first race was cold and cloudy, and the twenty-five single and twin-cylinder competitors practised among the bustle of regular traffic, much of it horse-drawn, on the untarred roads of the fifteen-mile St John's Course. Collier recalled:

> Originally the race was intended for purely touring machines exactly as offered for sale to the public; although there was no cc limit a much more effective limit was imposed by a petrol consumption maximum of 90mpg.... I can still recall the worrying dread of using more than the meagre allowance of petrol that was measured out carefully to each competitor at the start and again at half distance when a stop for refuelling was compulsory.[2]

With engines spluttering, the riders made their way to Tynwald Hill, where crowds had gathered to watch the start of the race. Fowler was suffering from the effects of an abscess on his neck, which was still heavily bandaged. He recalled in his record of the event fifty years afterwards that he was far from at his physical peak; indeed on reflection he felt that he was in no fit state to ride that day, for he was in a rather run down and nervous condition. However, just before the start a friend of his fetched him a glassful of neat brandy tempered with a little milk. This pepped him up, and he set off full of hope and Dutch courage.

Fellow competitors had warned him that his 700cc Norton bike was dangerously incompatible with the course. Its spring forks and the sheer length of the bike's wheel base, his rivals believed, would make it almost impossible for Rem to negotiate corners. His response was bullish, and he later stated that he answered his detractors in emphatic fashion by coming home in first place. His arch rival Billy Wells entered the race on a Vindec, but Rem was ready for his challenge; aside from his nerve tonic he set off on the 158-mile journey with just a spanner and four spare spark plugs – all of which would be needed – stuffed inside his coat.

Part of today's TT circuit, between Ballacraine and Kirk Michael, covers the same course as that race in 1907. Starting at St John's, the riders turned hard left at Ballacraine, before turning sharp left again back to Peel once they reached Kirk Michael, at the bend known as the Devil's Elbow. In Peel they turned left once more back to St John's. The biggest challenge on the course was undoubtedly Creg Willey's Hill, where in those days the road was narrow and winding. Most of the machines, apart from the two Triumphs, were also equipped with pedals, and the usual approach to this apparently unassuming gradient (which nevertheless represented a disproportionate challenge) was to open the throttle wide at Glen Helen and build up as much speed as possible, then pedal the last few yards. The Devil's Elbow was also a treacherous part of the course if approached too fast, and many a rider came unstuck there. The race was run over ten laps of the 15-mile 1,439-yard course, totalling some 158 miles. However, more than a century of infrastructure investment means that the quality of the road surface is now markedly different. The highway in 1907 was not metalled, and the surface was loose and gritty. In dry weather, passing traffic was apt to stir up clouds of dust, so the TT organisers decided that the best course of action was to spray this stretch of road with an acid solution from a water cart. This had unexpected effects. Not only did the acid fail to settle the swirling clouds of dust, but it also burned holes in the riders' clothing. Triumph competitor Jack Marshall (who, incidentally, also claimed to have won if stoppages were taken into account) remembered that the fine powdery surface presented another hazard:

> Overtaking was extremely difficult, not to say dangerous. One charged blindly into a cloud of dust and hoped that there would be a clear road ahead on the other side of it, and that the cause of the dust would not wobble or swerve as one went past.[3]

Corrosion, however, was probably the least of Rem Fowler's problems during the race. He encountered so many issues changing tyres, plugs and belts that at one stage he decided enough was enough and called it a day. It was not until a spectator informed him that not only that he was leading his class, but that he was also a massive half an hour ahead of Billy Wells, that he gleefully set off again with his initial gusto restored. Rem almost stopped again when faced with what he described as his most exciting moment. He recalled:

> About halfway through the race, as I approached the Devil's Elbow... I saw clouds of black smoke on the hill ahead of me. As I rounded the bend, there in the middle of the road was a machine, well alight, with flaming oil and petrol all over the road. I had to make up my mind instantly whether to obey the the violent flag-wagging of the Boy Scout on duty and stop, or to take a chance and dash through it. Realising that I had a good chance of winning, I decided to make a dash for it. The Boy Scout and others standing by were naturally taken by surprise, and only just got out of the way in time as I vanished into the flames. The chief risk actually was of hitting the burning machine, which was hidden in flames and smoke.

However, I managed to dodge it, and got through OK – all I felt was the hot blast. But I was very pleased to be on my way again, none the worse for what might have been a very nasty mess-up.[4]

Charlie Collier, meanwhile, was having difficulties of his own, and remembered:

My mount for this first TT was a single geared ohv single-cylinder two-port Matchless of 432cc, with all controls on the tank sides. Imagine having to remove one's hand from the bars for every change of ignition, air or throttle, and even for operation of the hand oil pump!... Imagine also coasting down the steeper inclines with the throttle closed and valve raised in order to conserve petrol and using the smallest possible throttle opening throughout for the same reason – the speed of 38mph was not so bad. So far as I was concerned there were no incidents in the race worthy of recording. I started No.4 together with my brother No.3, starting then being in pairs, and apart from passing two riders, Nos 1 and 2, and a few stranded competitors, I did not meet anybody from start to finish.[5]

Collier wins the 1907 TT. Inset: *Collier aboard a Matchless machine, built at the family's Plumstead works. (Manx National Heritage)*

The victory of the Matchless did not go uncontested by its competitors. Norton protested against Charlie Collier's pedal assist and, in its post-TT advertising, made much of Rem Fowler's bad luck, which they said had deprived the Birmingham rider of the overall win that his fastest lap suggested might have been his. Triumph, for whom Jack Marshall had traded the lead with Charlie Collier before finishing second in the single-cylinder race, claimed that it had made the fastest time when stops for repairs were deducted. Echoes of this early TT controversy can still be heard. Nevertheless, Collier and Fowler collected the £25 cheques awarded to the winners of each class. Collier had achieved 94.5mpg over the course of the race, and despite the Norton's fast lap he had been steadily drawing out his lead and was nearly fourteen minutes ahead by the end.

So the first of the twenty-five greatest Isle of Man TT machines is Charlie Collier's Matchless, but nothing is known for certain of the eventual fate of the machine, which appears to have been lost to history. One rumour has it that it ended its days in the foundations of a building. While the Collier brothers were always modest about their achievements, and Matchless as a firm never capitalised on the publicity that this first TT win might have brought them, Norton were less reticent. They never missed an opportunity for many years afterwards to trumpet the fact that one of their machines had won the first-ever TT race. Perhaps this is why, along with the fact that a machine claimed to be that ridden by Fowler in 1907 (though disputed by some) survives in the National Motorcycle Museum at Birmingham, it is Fowler's name which is forever associated in the public consciousness with that first race, and not Charlie Collier.

Chapter 2

580cc Indian twin (rider Oliver Godfrey) 1911

The second machine in this virtual hall of fame comes from one of the most famous motorcycle manufacturers in the world, and one whose all-too-brief flirtation with the TT produced impressive results at the time. This firm, the American-based Indian brand, was among the earliest competitors when motorcycle racing began on the Isle of Man, but the interest of the company in the event sadly waned after the First World War. Nevertheless, their achievements in the 1911 TT remain at the forefront of motorcycle racing history, and indeed are part of TT legend. It is the machine ridden to success that year by British rider Oliver Godfrey that forms the subject of this next chapter.

The Indian Motorcycle Company was originally founded by George M. Hendee in 1897, as the Hendee Manufacturing Company, in order to manufacture bicycles. The brand name 'American Indian', quickly shortened to just 'Indian', was adopted by Hendee from 1898 onwards, because it gave better product recognition in export markets. Oscar Hedstrom joined the company in 1900 as chief engineer. Both Hendee and Hedstrom were former bicycle racers and manufacturers, and they teamed up to produce a motorcycle with a 1.75bhp, single-cylinder engine in Hendee's home town of Springfield, Massachusetts. Four years after Hedstrom's arrival, the company introduced the deep red colour that would become Indian's distinctive trademark. In 1905, Indian built its first V-twin factory racer, and in following years made a strong showing in racing and record-breaking. Indeed, competition success played a big part in the company's rapid growth and spurred on technical innovation. Indian were moderately successful manufacturers in the early TT races, scoring a second place in 1909 and top-ten finishes in most years up to 1914, but 1911 was undoubtedly the pinnacle of their achievement.

The 1911 TT was significant because it saw the first use of the Mountain Circuit. The St John's course, which had been used since 1907, had fallen out of favour, as the residents of the western city of Peel objected to racers hurtling through their narrow streets. At the same time, the more innovative manufacturers (Indian in particular) had begun to use a chain rather than a leather belt drive between the engine and rear wheel. This gave them the capacity to tackle the steep gradient of Snaefell mountain and thus compete on what had previously been known as the 'four-inch course', because it had formerly been used by motorcars of four-inch cylinder capacity. As well as chain drives, there were various approaches among the different manufacturers to the thorny question of gearing, also essential for tackling gradients, with Indian again in the forefront. Overall, racing on the Mountain Circuit was as hazardous as on the St John's course, partly because of the poor condition of many of the Island's roads – many were little more than dusty dirt tracks, which turned into slippery mud slides when it rained – but also because of the added obstacles presented by sheep, and the gates across the road intended to keep them from straying.

For the first time the race was split into Junior and Senior events, with the 1911 Junior TT won by Percy Evans aboard a Humber machine. Three days later came the Senior, with no fewer than five riders supported by the Indian factory: flamboyant American racer Jake de Rosier, Arthur Moorhouse, Charles Franklin, Jimmy Alexander and Oliver Godfrey. Godfrey's father was an artist and painter who was also known as an engraver. Perhaps it was the search for work in this field which led him to depart for Australia (and out of his son's life forever) prior to 1901. In April 1911, just before his big race, Oliver was living with his mother and his stepfather's family in Finchley (north-west London) and was employed as a motor spindler (a motor engineer). He had become interested in motorcycles, and it was probably though his connection with UK Indian concessionaire Billy Wells (also London-based) that he first became involved with the American firm. Wells also managed the racing team, and the 'technical advisor' was the Great White Chief of Indian himself, company engineer Oscar Hedstrom. Their cycles, special machines built at the Indian factory to comply with TT rules, were 580cc 'little twins' equipped with a two-speed transmission borrowed from the company's 1,000cc 'big twin' model, in order to cope with the demands of the hilly course.

The 187.5-mile Senior race in 1911 was billed as a Britain-versus-America showdown, with Charlie Collier of Matchless representing Britain, and the flamboyant de Rosier carrying the honour of the USA. This, however, was not the whole story, because the race was actually wide open, perhaps surprisingly so, with maybe a score of riders thought by the pundits to have a chance of winning. As well as the Indian team and the Collier brothers, Philipp on the Scott machine was reckoned to be in with a fair chance, as well as the BAT-mounted trio of the Bashall brothers and H.H. Bowen, and the four Ariel riders, as well

Oliver Godfrey in Royal Flying Corps uniform, around 1916. (Royal Aero Club)

as Rudge and Triumph competitors who could not be discounted. Weather conditions on the day, Monday 3 July, were near-perfect, with sunshine and a light breeze, and the roads were dry and firm after three days of sunshine. The refuelling depots were at Ramsey, and the 'pits' on Quarterbridge Road (the term, now used in motor-racing worldwide, originated here), while the start line in those days was at Woodlands, on the slightly inclined ground at the middle part of Bray Hill before the junction with Alexander Drive, where a large crowd of spectators had gathered. The Lieutenant Governor of the Island, Lord Raglan, was watching from the judges' hut.

The race began as a duel between Collier, who started to a great cheer from the crowd as his engine fired first time, and de Rosier, who was strikingly attired in black tights, running shoes and a light blue woollen hat. The American had already crashed several times in practice, but put in a perfect first lap and was the early leader of the race. Oliver Godfrey, described at the time as diminutive in stature, struggled at the start, pushing his machine for some yards before it fired, but once in the saddle he accelerated away. De Rosier's magnificent form left Godfrey to battle it out with Collier, who was struggling his way around the treacherous course, for second place. The uneven and loose surface at the top of Bray Hill was almost Collier's undoing as he flew through to complete his first lap.

To those in the press box, Godfrey, who was born in London in 1887, seemed to be going faster than Collier, though stopwatches proved that the pair were on exactly the same time. As the race progressed, punctures, plug troubles and other mishaps thinned the field considerably. The second lap saw Collier push de Rosier into second place. The fourth lap brought the most drama, with Collier stopping to mend a puncture and de Rosier halting at Ramsey for twenty minutes with inlet valve problems. By the fourth lap, Godfrey was leading, though afterwards both he and Collier admitted that they were not aware of their respective positions. On the final lap, Godfrey was noted as travelling at tremendous speed, but his rear tyre was almost flat. It was not to be a stopwatch finish, as Godfrey beat Collier by one minute and three seconds. More drama followed after the race, as de Rosier was disqualified for using spare parts which he had not carried on the machine, and Collier likewise was outlawed for taking on fuel at an unauthorised depot. This promoted third-placed man Charles Franklin to second, and gave third place to A.J. Moorehouse, giving Indian a 1-2-3.

Godfrey simply rode consistently and well enough to finish the race without falling and with enough speed to beat Charlie Collier, even had he not been disqualified. The *Ramsey Courier* noted that:

> The inclusion of some of the most noted cyclists of the day throughout the world fairly entitled the event to the honour of a 'derby' in its way, and the Indians, captained by Jake de Rosier, fully sustained their reputation, coming out of the ordeal at the top of the tree. With flying colours... all the Indians rode splendidly, and notwithstanding Rosier's debacle, his confreres Godfrey, Franklin and Moorhouse came to the forefront, and were the first bunch of winners in at the finish.

> Godfrey's appearance on the last round was the signal for quite a furore, to the accompaniment of a lively tattoo on petrol tins from supporters of the Indians, punctuated with cries of 'Good old Godfrey'. Franklin too, who followed, came in for a hearty and similar ovation.[6]

In a rather upbeat report of the race issued by the Hendee Company and reprinted in the 1912 Indian UK sales catalogue, Godfrey was described as:

> ...small in size, but a bunch of muscles and nerves and a magnificent rider. He has ridden in the Tourist Trophy race before, and in many other prominent events, but never had a really first-class mount until this year.[7]

The Indian machine he rode, meanwhile, was described as being in absolutely perfect condition, and could have repeated the performance without the slightest difficulty, as there was not the most trifling adjustment necessary. Not surprisingly, Indian were delighted at the publicity (and sales) that a result like this could bring them. However, in some quarters of the British motorcycle fraternity there was great consternation that locally produced machines had been bested on home turf, and the event became known as the 'red Indian massacre'. Godfrey's winning feat established a number of 'firsts', including the first-ever clean sweep by a factory team, the first TT win by a foreign manufacturer, the first Senior TT win on the Mountain Course, and the first Mountain Course race record (though Frank Applebee's Scott set the first Mountain Course lap record).

Applebee, who was Godfrey's boyhood friend, later became his business partner and the two ran a motorcycle dealership named Godfrey's at 208 Great Portland Street, London. With the outbreak of the First World War in August 1914, Godfrey was commissioned into the Royal Flying Corps as an officer. There was a strong link at this time between motorcycle technology and aviation, and with their knowledge of spark plugs and cylinders many of the British TT pioneers likewise found themselves as pilots on the Western Front. Godfrey was posted to No.27 Squadron, flying Martinside Elephants, and in September 1916 the squadron was on a bombing mission near Cambrai when it was intercepted by a fighter group led by the infamous Red Baron, Manfred von Richthofen. Several British aircraft were shot down, including Godfrey's. His body was never recovered.

Some confusion exists about the fate of Godfrey's 1911 Indian. It was at one point believed to be in the Science Museum, London. However, an ambiguity in the description, which had implied it was the winner of the 1911 TT, was subsequently resolved: the wording should have stated that a machine *of this type* won the race, not this particular example. Another potential clue lies in the programme for an exhibition of historic motorbikes held at the Villa Marina, Douglas, in 1957 to mark the fiftieth anniversary of the TT races. Here again an Indian motorcycle was included, and was stated to be the winner of the 1911 Senior TT. However, if this was indeed the case, then the machine has subsequently vanished into obscurity. Though none of these special machines

Dave Roper's replica of the 1911 model Indian, as used by Oliver Godfrey. (Author's collection)

have survived intact to the present day, former Antique Motorcycle Club of America president and vintage bike collector Peter Gagan located a 580cc Indian racing engine in England some years ago, which may have powered one of the original 1911 TT machines. Unfortunately the records to verify this hypothesis do not exist, but Peter decided to use the engine as the basis for a replica using a 1911 Indian frame and transmission. Since no drawings of the TT bikes exist, frame modifications and exhaust pipes had to be fabricated according to photos of the originals. The replica Indian racer bears number twenty-six, the number on the bike that Oliver Godfrey rode to first place in 1911, and it was brought to the Isle of Man in 2011 by American classic and vintage racer Dave Roper to celebrate the centenary of the event.

Even though the actual machine probably no longer survives, Godfrey's Indian takes its place as number two in the pantheon of the greatest TT racing motorcycles. The winner of one of the most dramatic and talked-about of the early TT races, it represents the high watermark of Indian success at the Isle of Man. Hedstrom retired from the company in 1913, and Hendee resigned as president three years later. After this, the company seems to have moved in a different direction, and was less interested in racing (in the Isle of Man, at any rate). In 1911, however, they were at the forefront of motorcycle design and technology, which was borne out by their stunning performance in the first-ever Mountain Senior.

Chapter 3

500cc Douglas sidecar outfit (riders Freddie Dixon/Walter Denny) 1923

The first sidecar race at the TT was run in 1923, and it immediately established itself as one of the most exciting of the meeting. Indeed, the *Isle of Man Times* described that first race as 'the most thrilling ... in the world'. For sheer spectacle, little can beat sidecar racing, and even in those early days it was obvious that to be successful both teamwork and mutual trust between rider and passenger were essential. Thus our next TT titan is the grandfather of all subsequent TT sidecar outfits – the combination used by the legendary Freddie Dixon (and passenger Walter Denny) to win that first-ever event. It exemplified Dixon's ability both as an engineer and as a racer, and in many ways its innovative nature foreshadowed subsequent machines that appear later in this book, such as Dave Molyneux's sidecar outfit from 2003.

Sidecars were a popular early form of family transport, and by simply bolting the wheeled car onto a standard motorcycle, the Edwardian rider could immediately add versatility to his machine, enabling him to transport additional passengers or extra goods. Motorcycle and sidecar combinations had seen a great deal of service during the First World War, bringing them to wider attention, and it was at the third post-war meeting that a sidecar race first appeared on the TT programme. It was to be run over three laps of the Mountain Course, on the Wednesday afternoon of race week, immediately after the Lightweight race. One of the pioneers of the event was 'Fast Freddie' Dixon (born Frederick William Dixon on 21 April 1892 at 31 Alliance Street, Stockton-on-Tees). Freddie left school at the age of thirteen and went to work in a cycle shop, soon moving to Kit McAdam's Garage in Yarm Lane as an apprentice mechanic. He acquired his first motorcycle in 1909 and within a year was competing in speed and hill climb events in and around Stockton-on-Tees. In 1912, at the age of nineteen, he competed in the Isle of Man TT races for the first time on a Cleveland Precision motorcycle, but sadly the machine was not up to the challenge, and in the Senior he was forced to retire. However, Freddie's disillusion with this standard 'off the shelf' machine, and its lack of suitability for the task in hand, inspired his passion for tinkering with and improving standard or basic models.

During the First World War, Freddie spent four years in the RASC (Royal Army Service Corps), rising to the rank of staff sergeant. On returning to civilian life he went into business for himself at Park Garage on Linthorpe

MR F. DIXON

Freddie Dixon, seen here on a 1920s cigarette card. (Author's collection)

Road, Middlesbrough, though he continued to compete in motorcycle races, with placings in various race categories throughout the 1920s. He continued to persevere with the Indian brand in solo races during those early post-war years at the TT, but it was aboard a 500cc Douglas that he chose to compete in that first sidecar race. Dixon wrote later:

> My win in the 1923 Sidecar TT rather stands out in my memory as a kind of joke with a lucky break in it. Having arranged to ride a Douglas outfit in this race I thought I had better get down to the factory in Bristol to see what sort of a job was being prepared. I found they were busy making up a job with a leaning body and I didn't much care for it. As there was only about a week before we must leave for the Island, I was quite a bit worried, and after one or two sleepless nights, I dreamt of that comic thing – the 'banking sidecar'.
>
> It seemed a hopeless proposition to get one made up in time, but I thought 'nothing venture – nothing gain[sic]', and promptly turned my sex appeal on to Bill Bailey, who was in charge at the time. He laughed when I mooted the idea of getting one through in time, but I eventually persuaded him that it might be done and he placed the whole resources of the factory at my disposal.
>
> There was no time for drawings so I did a quick bit of chalking on the Experimental Shop floor, and with a few willing helpers, and not bothering about sleep, we knocked up a complete sidecar with an all-metal body having a rolling seat, as used by some oarsmen. Nothing needed modification, and my first passenger – the one and only Alec Bennett – was enthusiastic at the tricks we could get up to.[8]

Dixon's design was simplicity itself, and it combined tremendous strength with the advantage that it did not produce a fixed bank, but one that could be adjusted by the passenger. It took Dixon only ten days to build up his TT-winning frame once the idea came to him. It is clear that nothing particularly complicated was used, and the design was quickly patented by Dixon and the chief engineer at Douglas, S.L. Bailey, with a view to potentially turning it into a commercial proposition.

The adjustment principle did not rely upon any swivelling joints, ball joints, universal joints or similar devices. Dixon's plan was simply to raise and lower the sidecar wheel. Thus, if he raised the sidecar wheel spindle, the outfit naturally dropped towards the nearside, for of course it would not balance with the wheel in the air! As it dropped it canted over, and so the crew obtained a natural banked angle, the sidecar and driving wheels being parallel, but canted over to a degree determined by the amount of lift given to the sidecar wheel. Similarly, if the sidecar wheel bearing were dropped, the frame was raised, and so the outfit tended to lean towards the offside, required for turning to the right. The only extra moving part on the outfit was the arm on which the sidecar wheel was mounted.

Dixon's frame, as well as being simple, was also immensely strong. It was attached to his machine at three points, and the chassis was triangulated. All the connections were at footrest level, there being no saddle seat tie rod or connection below the head. Two of the connections were large diameter, and passed right through the duplex Douglas frame. The third transverse member was made hollow and formed the axle of the sidecar wheel. On it rotated a seven-inch arm webbed for strength and carrying the sidecar wheel spindle. Passing through the hollow axle was a control rod, coupled with a lever arranged between the sidecar body and the machine. A second lever, also mounted on this rod, occupied a similar position on the nearside of the body. These levers raised or lowered the sidecar wheel, according to whether they were pushed forwards or backwards, and two were provided to enable the passenger to control the banking apparatus whether he was leaning over the back wheel of the machine, or over the sidecar wheel.

It required a considerable amount of strength to raise or lower the sidecar frame and the passenger's own weight by means of these levers, so Dixon arranged a spring balance effect on them, so that their operation was made a good deal easier. Ratchets and pawls made it possible for the levers to be locked in any suitable position, press-knobs being provided to release the pawls, as on motorcar handbrake levers.

A rod passing through the hollow axle operated the sidecar brake. The body was made of aluminium, sand blasted on its upper surface to prevent sun glare, and another typical 'Dixonish' gadget was a sliding seat for the passenger. The seat itself and its back were arranged on rollers, something after the manner of a seat in a rowing boat. The passenger could slide his body forward in the sidecar and thus move the back rest into a horizontal position so that he could lie flat, or slide backwards to raise the back of the seat, which enabled him to adopt a normal sitting position, the better to control the banking levers.

Dixon was one of the most careful mechanics who ever rode in a TT race. He did nearly all his work himself, and trusted nobody with his machines. Most motorcyclists of the day knew his little fads, such as a back rest on his saddle, footboards and so forth, but it is not generally known that he also employed two twist-grip controls, one on each end of the handlebars, on his sidecar machine, so that he could work his throttle when both hands were on the left-hand bar, while he was cornering to the left. Apart from throttle controls, he had a horror of wire cables and wherever possible he would employ rods. For instance, his sidecar brake was rod-operated, as were the ignition controls, extra air levers and oil pumps.

Freddie had made several other modifications to the motorcycle itself, one of which was to the oiling, which originally was a 'Total Loss' system. It was operated by means of a hand pump (with a lever on the right handlebar) contained in the oil tank below the engine. This could easily flood the engine with oil, so Freddie cut a large hole about an inch in diameter in both crankcase and tank, sealed the gap with a rubber ring, and let the oil drain back to the tank. Large breathers were added to cope with crankcase compression. It is not generally known that there was also an ingenious telltale metering valve for the oil supply. This was in the petrol tank near the front. When the spring-loaded pump was delivering, the telltale knob lifted. Rotating the knob brought a succession of different size holes into line with the outlet, ranging from almost nil to full-bore. The attention to detail in even the smallest areas was a credit to Dixon's engineering skill. No bolt was used where a tube and split pin could serve the same purpose, all bolts where it was permissible were hollow, all frame lugs were scarfed and tapered to the limit. To save weight, mudguards were made of aluminium, wheel rims were made of special alloy which made them very light, and extensive use of special steel alloys even permitted the rear wheel spindle to be 'waisted' down to 3/8" between threaded portions. Freddie takes up the story once again:

> We landed in the Isle of Man feeling very happy, but had a nasty shock when the scrutineers put the bar up and said we could not use such a dangerous contraption, and during the early practice period we had to have the works locked in the rigid position. However, my pleading availed, and we were allowed to use the gadget for one lap under close observation at different parts of the course. The job worked fine, and we carved quite a chunk off the lap record with my passenger, young Walter Denny, sitting in a perfectly normal manner.[9]

In fact Dixon set the lap record in practice and was the hot favourite to win the race, ahead of close rival Graham Walker (father of commentator Murray Walker), who was riding a Norton outfit. Dixon continues his account:

> The day of the race came with things looking very rosy and off we went. We very quickly passed those who had started before us. As it appeared

we had so much in hand, I eased up considerably, and Denny and I entertained each other up the Mountain singing 'We Won't be Home till Morning'.

A shock was coming for I had forgotten those behind, and suddenly there was a nasty scream and Harry Langman passed us. Mental calculation told me that we would really have to get our skates on now. Up went the wick and I soon re-passed him, not knowing whether he would need to stop for fuel, as we must do. I got that job over, and was just pushing off, when Harry came chasing through. He led me through Braddan Bridge, and we arrived there some two seconds later to find him upside down and sliding all over the place. We missed him, but I don't know to this day how it was done.

Breathing a sigh of relief, I kept the steam on, thinking there might be others I had miscalculated. More trouble was brewing, for as we took Hillbery on this – the last – lap, at somewhat hectic speed, the inner duplex frame tube suddenly snapped. The handlebar jamming on the body stopped a total collapse, but it was only by wangling the banking lever that we were able to hobble home and see the welcome chequered flag.[10]

They won the race by covering the three laps in 2 hours, 7 minutes 48 seconds, giving an average speed of 53.15mph, winning comfortably over Graham Walker and George Tucker. Harry Langman, although he crashed out, had still managed to set the fastest lap of the race on his Scott outfit. The *Isle of Man Times* was very supportive of the new event, stating that:

An exceedingly large number of thrills must have been afforded to the crowds round the Course by the spectacular performance of both riders and sidecar passengers. It was a race to test the will of the driver, the courage of the passenger, and the quality of the machine. The experiment of initiating a Sidecar Race for the improvement of that today rather unwieldy machine was a good one, worthy of encouragement. It is only by experience gained in such a thorough test as a road race that the faults of this article can be remedied and made safer for the general public to use.[11]

In spite of this vote of confidence, the sidecar races at the TT were initially shortlived – the class was dropped after 1925 after pressure from manufacturers, who believed that racing the outfits around the Isle of Man was not helping their image as a reliable and safe form of family transport!

Only in the 1950s would sidecar racing make a triumphant return to the Isle of Man. Dixon and Denny used the banking outfit at the three subsequent sidecar TT races, but were never able to repeat their success, retiring in each one. Dixon went onto even greater things, and remains the only man to have won a Tourist Trophy on two, three and four wheels. In motorcar racing, he set a lap record at Brooklands that was never beaten. His legacy on the Isle of Man lives on, in that one of the two sidecar mercuries for which drivers and passengers compete is named the Frederick Dixon trophy.

Some parts of the historic 1923 outfit still survive in the collection of vintage machines at Milntown, the majestic house just outside Ramsey on the Isle of Man. The machine on display there incorporates the original sidecar chassis with banking lever, for which the Milntown mechanic Bob Thomas made a replica sidecar body. The chassis had been given to Graham Walker when he was curator at the National Motor Museum at Beaulieu by Freddie Dixon himself. The original Douglas motorbike had been lost, so a replica was built by Bob (who happened to be a Douglas enthusiast) to the same specification as

The 1923 Dixon Banking Sidecar outfit, held in the Milntown collection. (Author's collection)

that used in 1923. The machine is now effectively co-owned by Milntown and Beaulieu, and may still be seen when the house is open to the public during the summer.

The Dixon/Denny outfit makes the grade as one of the greatest twenty-five TT machines, not simply as the first-ever winner of a sidecar TT race (though of course that is hugely important), nor even through its connection to the great Freddie Dixon, a true legend of British motorsport. Even more than both of these, it exemplifies the spirit of innovation that still characterises successful sidecar constructors at the TT races today, and it also set the benchmark for the trust and teamwork that is still to be found among the best sidecar crews on the Mountain Course.

Chapter 4

500cc Douglas
(rider Tom Sheard)
1923

Thomas Mylchreest (Tom) Sheard was a Manxman, born in Peel in 1889, and learned his trade as a mechanic with Messrs F.G. Wrigley and Co. in Birmingham, before taking a position as a mechanic with Athol Garage back on the Isle of Man. He later opened his own motor repair business in Victoria Road, Douglas. Sheard began competing on motorcycles before the First World War, and when racing returned to the Isle of Man in its aftermath he took up the sport once again. He was the first Manxman to win a TT, when he took first place in the 1922 Junior event, but for many observers at the time it was his win the following year in the Senior that was his crowning achievement. The motorcycle aboard which he took that victory, against some of the toughest opposition of the era, was a 500cc Douglas machine, and it is this which is the subject of the fourth chapter of this book.

The 1923 Senior race was also very much a drama in its own right, because it was the first wet TT. Despite terrible conditions at some places on the course, racing went ahead. The idea of rescheduling or even abandoning the race due to bad weather was simply not considered. The forty-eight runners who lined up at the start that day in 1923 listened in miserable silence to the official announcement: 'Rain all around course and thick mist on the Mountain.' The dismal weather, however, had the unprecedented effect of levelling the playing field – those on 350cc machines were actually quite pleased, as it meant that ease of handling would probably count for more than maximum speed, while other strong riders who might otherwise have been expected to win were genuinely worried, never having raced in the wet before. Many lowered their tyre pressures in order to give themselves more contact area with the road, and therefore more grip. Lined up on the starting grid alongside Sheard were Alec Bennett, arguably the most successful rider of the 1920s and also Douglas-mounted, Graham Walker, riding for Norton and again an incredibly successful and talented rider, Geoff Davison on a Triumph, and – making up the field somewhat because he was he was on unfamiliar Scott machinery – the great Stanley Woods, who had already triumphed in the Junior TT that week.

Nonetheless, despite the strength of the competition, Sheard was in with a strong chance, and not just because of his local knowledge. He was mounted aboard one of the best machines available at the 1923 TT. The Bristol-based Douglas factory was streets ahead of its competitors at the time, and had produced a superbly designed motorbike, created by the Australian engineer S.L. Bailey. Graham Walker, writing about the race some years later, was in no doubt that the Douglas motorcycles were the clear favourites to win the day:

> The great question in everyone's mind was 'how would the weather affect the Douglas' chances?' These revolutionary 68 x 68ohv horizontal twin models, designed and manufactured in less than five months, had come straight from S.L. Bailey's drawing board to the Island and had proved to be miles faster than anything else. Minor teething troubles had cropped up in the Junior race, but Dixon's sidecar victory, and the fact that the other two 'chairs' finished, proved the stamina of the engine department to be there. The short wheelbase, achieved by slinging the gearbox above the rear cylinder, and the amazingly low saddle position provided by the novel frame layout, gave excellent road holding, and the 28-inch wheels seemed to smooth out the bumps.[12]

The design was packed with innovative features. A separate oil sump acted as a draught deflector on to the rear cylinder; a handlebar control varied the flow of lubricant; the overhead valves, with their triple springs, were operated by wick-lubricated rockers, and there was a single-plate flywheel clutch. The British Research Association brakes, consisting of V-section fabric rings spoked to the wheels and operated by grooved aluminium shoes, were streets ahead of those on other makes. The synchronised twin carburettors drew their air supply through a huge aluminium box with a rearward facing inlet. The Douglas machines were also the lightest 500cc motorcycles in the race, only weighing 257lb – the same as the 350cc Sunbeams. However, using a completely new design was not without its drawbacks, as it would normally take at least twelve months of work just to get the design of something like a gearbox right. The machine Sheard rode had never been on the road, nor had the engine even been bench tested before it was sent to him! All the tuning and preparation of the machine was undertaken by Sheard himself, and the fact that it turned out to be so successful – at its first attempt – was a credit both to Bailey the designer, and to Sheard's methodical approach to setting it up.

As the race began, rider after rider encountered problems starting due to the dampness in the air. A steady stream then called in to the pits to change their goggles, before giving up on them altogether and going out with no eyewear. Sodden leathers, boots full of water, slimy gloves and stinging eyes made it a difficult race for everyone. After the first lap, Sheard was in fourth place. He was leading the race by lap two, and on the third circuit he was applauded by the crowd as he descended Bray Hill. By the third lap the weather was actually worsening, and those sections of road that had been newly coated with tarmac (a godsend in the hot dry conditions of the Junior race earlier in the week) became a deathtrap as bikes skidded on them. Several riders went straight on at Signpost Corner, including Sheard. In an account later published in *Motor Cycling* magazine, he wrote:

> The mist on the mountain was simply awful and, in spite of my being a local man and knowing the roads well, I was often at sea, especially on the corners immediately after the Bungalow. The first time round Creg ny Baa, I nearly put myself out of the race, for I misjudged the corner and overshot it, taking to the grass and skidding completely round in order to save myself. I also overshot Signpost Corner and had to take the slip road for over 100 yards, owing to the deceptive visibility. Many of the competitors were riding with their goggles up, but I dared not raise mine, for I knew that if I did so, the rain and mud would collect inside and render them useless...[13]

At the end of the fifth lap, Sheard was leading by nearly three minutes, but nothing is ever certain in a TT race, and he soon began to experience difficulties due to the weather, with a front plug which began cutting out in the curtain of water thrown up from the Mountain Road. Braking problems were also a distinct possibility and on some other machines they failed totally. Sheard used his as sparingly as possible and in fact used the inertia of the engine to slow himself down when coming into the pits, but he later reported that they were still working effectively even at the end of the race. Nevertheless, in spite of all these difficulties he crossed the line as winner at an average speed of 55.55mph, slower than the winning speed in the Junior race, which had been run in ideal conditions. An exhausted Sheard was helped to dismount by members of the Manx Motor Cycle Club, then carried shoulder high to the rest tent. At the subsequent prize presentation at the Palace Hotel, he received, along with his silver replica trophy, an engraved watch, presented by the Manx Automobile Club. He wrote later:

> I found the Douglas very comfortable at speed, and finished much fresher than last year... My tyres gripped splendidly and I could corner almost as fast as I could have done had the roads been dry, although, of course greater care was needed... It was a good race and I am very glad for Douglas's sake, that I was able to pull it off, for I think the machine's performances, considering that they were a new and untried design, was nothing short of marvellous.[14]

Some idea of the impact that Sheard's win had on the people of the Isle of Man comes from the fact that immediately afterwards, all of the local children who were playing at motorbike racers on their pushbikes wanted to have his number 2 as their number plate, and nothing else would do! It was even said that a Manx Sunday School teacher used his win as a parable, telling his class that this was an example of what could be achieved through sheer hard work and thorough preparation. There can be no doubt that for the people

Tom Sheard rounds Ramsey Hairpin aboard the Senior TT-winning Douglas, 1923. Inset: an exhausted Sheard is carried shoulder-high at the end of the race. (Manx National Heritage)

of the Island it was a David versus Goliath victory – one of their own had taken on and beaten the best riders in the world. In the weeks that followed, the Manx Motor Cycle Club held a dinner in Sheard's honour. A toast to him drew rousing cheers and applause, and the president spoke of his pluck and endurance, as well as his popularity. Sheard, modest as ever, quietly thanked the club for their kindness in staging the reception.

Today the Sheard motorcycle from 1923 is lovingly preserved and cared for by his family in Douglas. It is occasionally seen at rallies and parades, and has previously been on display at the Manx Museum on the Island. So why does the Tom Sheard motorcycle make the top twenty-five? Well, this in part due to the fact that the 1923 Douglas was a classic machine in its own right, and was technically far superior to most of its competitors that year; but Sheard's Douglas also has a significance for the Isle of Man that transcends this. His success in winning the Senior against some of the toughest opposition of his day was an incredible achievement, as commentators at the time recognised, and probably outshines his previous win, important in itself

The 1923 Senior TT-winning Douglas machine, ridden by Tom Sheard. (Manx National Heritage)

as the first for a Manxman. More important than all of this, however, is the machine's outstanding provenance. Several earlier TT-winning machines are claimed to survive in motorcycle museums in the UK. In most cases, however, there are serious question marks over their historical integrity. Indeed, one of these other machines was virtually destroyed and rebuilt from the ground up in recent years. The Sheard motorcycle has remained in the possession of his family since the day he crossed the finishing line, making it probably the oldest *undisputed* TT-winning machine still in existence.

Chapter 5

500cc Norton
(rider Harold Daniell)
1938

The Birmingham-based firm of Norton Motors has a special place in the history of the Isle of Man TT, and indeed in the history of the British motorcycle industry. Norton was and still is undoubtedly the most famous British motorcycle marque of all time. To his everlasting glory Rem Fowler rode a Norton to win the twin-cylinder class in the inaugural TT race in 1907, and by the late 1920s and 1930s the firm had come to dominate the event. Much as Honda would create so much TT history in the 1980s and 90s, so in the 1930s the record book was very much written by Norton. The redesigned camshaft motor introduced in 1930 was incredibly successful, and the basic design of single-cylinder, sturdy crank case and through bolts to hold down head and barrel remained more or less the same until 1961, giving Norton a string of victories as this one basic design was steadily improved upon. In 1931 the 80mph barrier on the Isle of Man was broken by Jimmy Simpson aboard a 500cc Norton, and in 1937 the lap record on the Island was pushed beyond the 90mph mark by Freddie Frith riding the same make. However, it is the record-breaking machine of another Norton rider that concerns us in this chapter.

Harold Daniell, a motorcycle dealer and mechanic from south London, hardly looked like a two-wheeled racing star. He was short sighted and wore glasses (he was turned down for active service in the Second World War due to his poor eyesight), but he took his physical fitness seriously in an era when few other riders did so. He had been a competitor at the Isle of Man TT since 1934, having previously competed in the Manx Grand Prix. In his early years he campaigned his own well-used Norton, but his secret weapon was his brother-in-law, Norton wizard Steve Lancefield. Lancefield was a genius with Norton engines, and in his workshop in his front room he tweaked and tuned them to squeeze out extra power. 1938 was to be a significant year for Daniell, because it was the first time he had appeared as an official Norton factory rider.

It is the machine with which he contested that year's seven-lap Senior race, held in near perfect conditions, that is at the heart of this chapter. As Norton did not compete in the following year's TT as a factory team, it represents the pinnacle of the firm's pre-war development under their renowned race team manager, Joe Craig.

Before the race itself there had been much speculation about the outcome, which was by no means a foregone conclusion. The Velocette team presented a strong challenge, and with Stanley Woods riding for them victory was certainly a possibility. The other big threat to Norton came from the BMW team, at this time effectively an extension of the German state and with all the resources it required provided by the Nazi regime, in pursuit of a propaganda victory. Top German rider Karl Gall had been injured in practice, but Georg Meier and Jock West, the second and third BMW riders, also presented a challenge. Certainly on paper the Germans were up on power: the turbocharged BMW Kompressor boxer twin of 1938 produced 68bhp, while the normally aspirated factory Nortons of this era produced around 50bhp. The British had other advantages, however, and the road-holding properties of the Nortons were probably greater. The first spring-framed Norton had appeared at the 1937 Manx Grand Prix, and Harold Daniell stated after the 1938 Senior race that the new telescopic front forks allowed much later braking into corners than the girder forks on the machine he had ridden in 1937. Although the BMWs of Meier and West had hydraulically damped telescopic forks, they were less effective over the bumpy road surface than the Norton equivalents. At the end of practice week, however, it was still wide open, and a less-than-convincing performance by Norton in the Junior race earlier in race week kept the thousands of spectators on the Island guessing.

The 1938 Senior TT took place on Friday 17 June, and there was early drama when Georg Meier retired shortly after crossing the start line with a melted spark plug, leaving only Jock West to fly the Swastika banner for the German team. Daniell was at first mindful of what had happened in the Junior race earlier in the week. He had seized his motor on the third lap, so in the Senior he rode carefully for the first few miles in order to give the engine a chance to properly warm up. However, as a result he began seeing frantic pit boards from the Norton team urging him to use more speed. When he stopped in the pits he was given a pep talk by an irate Joe Craig, who informed him in no uncertain terms that he was a good half a minute behind Stanley Woods and that he had better do something about it! Daniell wrote afterwards:

The end of the fourth lap was really the turning point for me. My fifth lap took 25.5 – just over the 90 mark – and I was really driving the model. We went better still in the sixth lap, and though I didn't know it until later, of course, beat the 25 minutes for the first time, with a lap in 24.57. At the end of the sixth lap I was given the signal '1 +4', which meant that I was leading by four seconds. I didn't know that I had beaten the lap record, and I certainly didn't intentionally 'go' for it on the last lap. But that pit signal had shown me that it was bound to be a very close thing and I just went on driving the machine up to the 'maximum permissible revs', with the result that my last lap was the fastest of the day... And, believe it or not, I took no more risks on that lap than on any other.[15]

Despite the fact that he must have been tiring as the race drew to a close, on the sixth lap Daniell, perhaps drawing on reserves of strength derived from his fitness regime, pushed his Norton on to post the first-ever lap under 25 minutes – 90.75mph – putting him in the lead by five seconds. Instead of coasting home, however, on lap seven he really wound the Norton up and this final lap was even faster – an unprecedented 24 minutes and 52.6 seconds, an average of 90.99mph. That figure stood as the outright TT record for twelve years. Daniell wrote afterwards:

I was now riding all out and the only way to improve my speed was to thrash the motor. I had been driving on the rev counter, and knowing these instruments are far from reliable, I decided to drive by 'feel'. This proved successful and at lap six my signal at Ramsey was a large W with -5 underneath. I was pleased to receive a signal at Ramsey at last – apparently I was in the race after all! But the W meant that Woods was leading, and that was not going to be a very popular result with the Bracebridge Street firm. I wondered where Freddie [Frith] was lying – actually we were dead heated in second place. On my last lap past the pits my signal was '2ⁿᵈ -3' with frantic waving to supplement the sign... On the last lap Ramsey Signal was '1 -5'and I nearly fell off with excitement. I calculated that now I was in the lead I had only to maintain my speed and concentrate on avoiding mistakes – and then it would be in the bag! Actually the final lap proved to be my fastest... Woods was still on the mountain when I finished and they were anxious moments waiting for him to come in. Looking back at the results, it is clear that the turning point of the race was in the fourth lap, which included the time taken at the pit stop for fuel and oil. This shows how important teamwork is while replenishing.[16]

Daniell continued his account with a theory of why his performance improved so dramatically towards the end of the race:

One thing that counts a lot, of course, is the weight of the machine towards the end of a race, when the tank is getting empty. Our tanks that year held approximately five gallons of petrol and we could just do four laps on a full tank – actually I found later that I finished with so little petrol in the tank there was scarcely enough to provide a sample for the examiners! Now petrol weighs approximately eight pounds a gallon, so five gallons weighs forty pounds. In other words, on a four-lap run the machine gets ten pounds lighter on each lap, and the important thing is that this weight reduction takes place at the top of the bicycle. So you not only get a lighter machine with better acceleration and braking, but you get a model which handles much better as well. All in all, therefore, it is only reasonable that the last lap should be your best, provided that the model is functioning OK and that you are not getting tired.[17]

Sometimes detractors have claimed that the only reasons Daniell's lap record stood as long as it did were the seven-year wartime hiatus, when there was no racing on the Isle of Man, and the fact that post-war riders were restricted to inferior pool petrol. However, it should perhaps also be borne in mind that Daniell's record was unbroken by either Jock West or Georg Meier, with their much-improved supercharged BMWs, in the 1939 Senior TT. When the record did eventually fall, it took a rider of the calibre of Geoff Duke to break it.

One little-known fact about the 91mph Norton was that it featured specially strengthened footrests. These were uniquely made for Harold Daniell, as at the TT and elsewhere he had a habit of breaking standard footrests; he was quite a heavily built individual. At the 1938 Manx Grand Prix in September, Johnny Lockett was riding Steve Lancefield's private Norton, and he also had a footrest problem. Lancefield, as noted, was Harold Daniell's brother-in-law and the works Norton was then at Lancefield's workshop. Lancefield sent a telegram home and asked that the footrests be taken off the Daniell Norton and sent over to the Isle of Man as soon as possible; they were quickly put in an aeroplane that was bound for the Island. After Johnny Lockett used them, finishing second in the Senior Manx Grand Prix, they were taken off and labelled to be returned to Harold Daniell's Norton. This was never done, and they remained for a number of years in Johnny Lockett's garage. Today they are in a private collection.

So what became of the rest of the all-conquering 1938 Norton? No one seems sure. It certainly does not seem to be in any of the obvious museums or collections. One curious fact, however, might intrigue motorcycle historians. A few years ago, a large collection of Lancefield and Daniell papers and photographs came up for auction, after Lancefield's widow died. It was

Harold Daniell aboard the the 1938 Norton, on which he achieved the 'lap at 91'. (Author's collection)

rumoured that the house clearance firm which dealt with the estate had found a motorbike rusting in a shed, though what became of it was unclear. Was it the 1938 Senior TT winner? We may never know, but regardless of what became of it, the Daniell Norton put in what was probably the most impressive performance of any machine at the TT prior to the Second World War, and easily earns its place as the fifth in the top twenty-five TT machines.

Chapter 6

350cc Velocette KTT (rider Stanley Woods) 1939

Dubliner Stanley Woods was undoubtedly the greatest TT rider of the pre-1939 era. He was the first rider to reach ten wins (an incredible achievement, when one considers that for most of the era in which he rode, there were only three solo races each year) and he might well have gone on to greater success had the Second World War not curtailed his career. Woods was also a great character, with an easy-going charm that made him a firm favourite with TT spectators. He was known as the 'Toffee Man' because of his habit of giving away toffees made at his factory in Dublin, particularly to the Scouts who manned the scoreboard at the Grandstand. It is the machine he first rode in the 1937 Junior TT, and which would go on to win both the 1938 and 1939 events, which is the subject of this chapter.

Stanley Woods exemplified a new generation of professional factory riders who emerged in the years after the First World War. It is no exaggeration to say that these men were the sporting superstars of their day. In an era when footballers were paid the equivalent of factory workers' wages, professional motorcycle racers were the sporting elite – fêted in the press and lionised by the public. Woods's style of riding was graceful and elegant. He sat well up in the saddle even for fairly fast curves, and took the slower ones much as if he was riding a horse.

Woods had ridden for a number of different manufacturers since his career began, but by 1936 he was riding for the Birmingham firm of Veloce, based at Hall Green. He had previously enjoyed a good relationship with Joe Craig at Norton, and during a stint with Italian firm Moto Guzzi found that managers and engineers would listen to his ideas and suggestions, even providing a translator to ensure easy communication between rider and engineer. This was not the case at Veloce, however, as Woods remembered many years later:

> ...If you made a suggestion to Velocette, you had to be able to substantiate it with figures. They would always try to prove you wrong. I was told that

T.T. RACING - STANLEY WOODS

Stanley Woods, seen here on a 1930s cigarette card. (Author's collection)

what I was trying to do, had not yet been done. Trying to win the TT at a higher speed than the previous year. So I said, 'How can you know by a guessing stick whether I'm right or wrong?' But you couldn't persuade them. Shocking people... A visit to Hall Green was a strange experience. You had to be a diplomat in the way you put a point over. They didn't like to think that somebody from outside would come and tell them what to do.

One morning I arrived at Hall Green about 10 o'clock and George Denley said, 'How long do you think you will be here?' and I said,

'I suppose I'll be here all day, nothing else to do.' And he said, 'In a few minutes now we'll go off to the board room for a cup of tea. Probably Mr Eugene, who's works manager, will be there. He'll take you round the factory and show you the latest production machines they've installed. In due course, we'll meet again in the board room for lunch. In the afternoon Harold Willis will probably take you down to the experimental department and see what's going on there. Around 4 o'clock we'll meet in the board room again for a cup of tea.'

Then he said, 'If you've any ideas about changing or doing anything, don't mention them until tea time. Then you should say – "I wonder what would happen if we did such and such?" Don't follow it up. Don't say any more, then in six weeks the idea will sprout'.[18]

He continued with a description of what he viewed as a backwards step by Veloce: dropping their twin-cam engine after a mechanical failure cost them the 1936 Junior TT:

The twin cam was marvellous. I reckoned the 1936 race was in my pocket. The only one I feared was Guthrie and I set my opening lap on what I reckoned he would be doing. I think I was four or five seconds behind at Sulby on the first lap, which suited me nicely. I was finding my way round, kind of business, but coming out of Sulby Bridge, on the first lap, the motor stopped with a broken Oldham coupling. We never got a chance to show our paces.

The biggest mistake they ever made was in the winter of 1936. They went crackers about the Aspin rotary valves after deciding to drop the twin camshaft engine because it had let me down in the Junior. There was nothing wrong with the engine. All they had to do was waist the vertical shaft to introduce a bit of flex in the drive, which they did later. But... the twin cam [was] scrapped. So it was back to the single cam for 1937... and they didn't actually find the speed until I think, the week before practice. It was as slow as ditch water. They didn't have my 350 engine ready until a week before. I never had the bikes myself, of course... Guthrie beat me by 7 minutes, but it might as well have been 10. They didn't re-introduce the double cam until after the war.[19]

Considering this lack of power, fourth place in the 1937 Junior TT was a creditable result for Woods and his machine. However, this motorcycle, which had shown little initial promise, would be developed by Veloce into a highly competitive TT-winning machine. Chief among the modifications that winter was an increase in the size of the inlet valve to that on their 500cc machine. In its final form the works 350 featured a number of modifications not present on Velocette production machines, including magnesium engine and gearbox case; long con rod with an oil feed to the little end; taller cylinder; additional pumps to clear oil from the top of the engine; waisted vertical shaft within an alloy tube; top and bottom bevel housings carrying roller bearings; ten-inch square cylinder head against nine-inch square on the production KTT; a valve-type shock absorber against the standard unit (which had failed in the past); special heavy-duty gearbox; final drive sprockets spliced to the mainshaft (following the failure of the mainshaft in the 1937 Ulster Grand Prix), and a cast-iron brake drum bolted to a magnesium front hub, giving improved braking. Woods remembered that this two-piece unit was so effective he could outbrake anyone. He commented modestly: 'Velocettes had come on in power in 1938 and I won the Junior for them in the Island, reasonably comfortably.'[20]

This, however, is far from being the whole story. The race began at 11am promptly on 13 June. Woods was third away, but climbed quickly through the field. By the time he reached Ramsey he was first on the road. By the end of the first lap Velocette factory duo Woods and Ted Mellors held first and second places respectively. Woods, however, was getting faster, and on his second lap equalled the class record held jointly by Freddie Frith and the late Jimmy Guthrie. On his third lap he broke it by two seconds. He led the race from start to finish, with an average speed of 84.08mph.

It was to be the following year that the real challenge came, from the German firms of BMW and DKW. In fact the Germans were now fielding what was effectively a 'national' team at the TT, with the individual German firms working together, with support from their government, with a view to winning on behalf of the Nazi regime. The Germans had first fielded a competitive team in 1938, but by 1939 they had an even more formidable weapon in the shape of the supercharged BMW, slated to contest the Senior. Before that could be decided, however, another challenge had to be faced. Monday 12 June was the date of the 1939 Junior TT, the first race of the week. The weather was generally good, with a fresh breeze and mostly sunny, with some drizzle at Ballacraine. Woods aboard the 350 Velocette was away first, to a great cheer from the crowd. Stanley himself recorded:

On race day, as zero hour drew near I admit I felt a bit nervy, but I was also supremely confident of being able to win. A grand feeling! At last the starter dropped his flag and off I went. As usual, I pushed much too far before dropping the clutch, but when I did the Velocette started at once. Down Bray Hill the engine seemed to rev up through the gears very quickly, and the same away from Quarter Bridge, Braddan and

Union Mills. Up the hill to Ballahutchin she peaked in third gear and took top gear long before her usual point. I congratulated myself on the foresight that had made me take special precautions to see that the oil was thoroughly heated during the warming up period.[21]

A correspondent at Union Mills meanwhile reported: 'As was only to be expected, Stanley Woods took the bends perfectly – in his usual nonchalant style and with no fearful appearance of hurry.'[22]

However, the spectators at Governor's Bridge were somewhat disappointed by Woods on this first lap, because it seemed that he was being cautious almost to the point of being slow. He faced stiff opposition from Freddie Frith (Norton), who was riding at tremendous pace, and from Fleischmann (DKW), and by the end of lap one Woods was down in fourth place. Another challenger, Harold Daniell, came off in Parliament Square and although he remounted he had slipped two places down the leaderboard. In fact, Woods was in difficulties early on in the race because of a faulty rev counter. The dial was telling him that he was at 7000rpm, the maximum that the engine could withstand. This was actually the second clock fitted to the bike – one had already failed in practice week – and so Woods chose to disregard this one as well and pushed to 7500rpm, which the 350cc engine took in its stride. By the second lap Woods was up to third place with a speed of 83.20mph, but localised rain made the road slippery between Ginger Hall and Ramsey. Choosing discretion over valour, Woods eased off a little in deference to the tricky conditions. After a 31-second pit stop he was on his way for the third lap, but received a nasty shock when told just how far off the pace he had actually been. He continued:

> It was about this time that I began to suspect the rev counter of trying to lead me up the garden path. Coming out of Union Mills I decided to let her rev until the valves bounced. Higher and higher went the revs and not till the clock registered just over 8000 did the valves start to float. And just at the usual point on the road, too. I had been deceived by a lying clock that registered 1000 revs out![23]

By the end of this lap, Woods was lying second. On lap four, the first-placed rider Frith retired at Ballaugh with engine trouble, and Woods was promoted to race leader. By now the rev counter had given up completely and he was riding purely on the sound of the engine. He was by no means out of danger:

> A spot of excitement on this last lap at Close Wood, near Sulby. Deschamps had parted company with his Norton on the grease under the trees. Before the road could be cleared I came along – at about 110mph. The road

here takes a series of bends – right, left, right, left. I do not shut off until I am round the first right, then I brake slightly and engage third gear. Thereafter, I accelerate through the remainder of the bends, emerging on the approach to Sulby Straight at almost peak revs in third. Quite a nice place to find the road blocked! And that is just what I might have done if it had not been for the quick action of a lady spectator. She was standing on the apex of the first left bend, inside the hedge, and as I approached she waved a red hat violently in front of me. It looked a bit too agitated to be merely enthusiasm, so I eased up considerably and picked a course past the fallen rider with ease.[24]

A late charge by Harold Daniell meant that the result was not a foregone conclusion, and with Daniell starting so far behind in the field, Woods sat for a full ten minutes in the paddock waiting for him to cross the line. He later described this as the worst few minutes of his entire career, but when both men had finished it transpired that Woods had won by eight seconds. On film footage shot at the time, Stanley can clearly be seen in the paddock anxiously looking for Daniell, his face lighting up after he finishes and the timings are confirmed. It was a result made all the more impressive by the fact that in the previous year's Belgian Grand Prix, while overtaking another competitor, Woods had been forced to run off the track and crashed, losing the first finger of his left hand as a result. By the 1939 TT the injury was healed, but the whole left hand was weakened and circulation in it was impaired, making it difficult for him to keep it warm.

The Lightweight race two days later was won by Benelli, and the news of the victory was cabled directly to Mussolini in Rome. On the Friday of race week came the second Axis propaganda victory when the Senior TT was won easily by Georg Meier aboard the supercharged BMW. To this machine the British manufacturers had no answer. Norton were already engaged on military contracts as Britain desperately rearmed. They fielded no factory team and handed their 1939 machines – one of which survives today as the Crosby Norton – to privateers. Velocette had attempted to counter the German challenge with their own supercharged Roarer twin. However, it did not arrive on the Isle of Man until the middle of race week. With most of British industry going over to war work it was impossible to get hold of special materials to to get any jobs done outside of the factory. Veloce knew that the bike was not going well, and that the supercharger was not producing enough pressure, and Woods rode it for only one lap of practice. Subsequently, Adolf Hitler congratulated Meier and promoted him. The Senior TT victory was, like the 1936 Berlin Olympics, a major publicity coup for the Nazis.

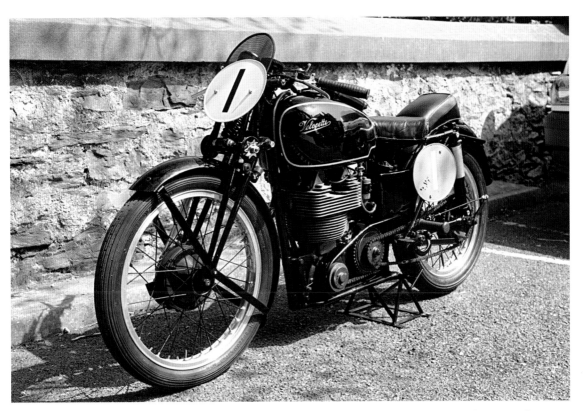

The Woods 350cc Velocette, winner in 1938 and 1939, as it is today, lovingly restored by the Rhodes family. (Manx National Heritage)

Thus the Junior TT victory in 1939 was not only a race win, but also a much-needed boost for British pride. It meant a great deal to the Veloce company, which with war looming was desperate to be looked upon favourably by the British public. The company had been founded by a German family and during the First World War had been viewed with deep suspicion, even hostility. The fact that they scored the only win for a British manufacturer at the 1939 TT was a great boost for them, even if (as he himself acknowledged) it was ironic that their rider was from the Irish Republic.

Throughout the war years the Woods machine languished at the Hall Green works, until 1947 when the TT finally returned. It was said, only half jokingly, that it was found on a scrap heap, dusted off and set up again! The machine was taken to the first post-war TT by Peter Goodman, son of the factory boss Eugene Goodman, and retained the pre-war central spring front fork and the Dowty rear suspension of Woods's day. The lack of improvement did not unduly worry the Velocette development engineer Mr Udall, who commented:

The machine was good enough to get round at 83-84 on petrol-benzole, and now that we are going on to tractor vaporizing fuel, the speed will be lower, so why worry?[25]

Using this poor-quality pool petrol, Goodman came home in seventh place in the 1947 Junior, a creditable performance. Some time after this, the machine was dismantled and its components distributed around the country. Many of the parts were subsequently located by renowned Velocette enthusiast Ivan Rhodes over a thirty-year period, and the machine was lovingly reassembled. Some components were stamped SW350 (for Stanley Woods), while others were stamped EM350 for his teammate Edward Mellors, reflecting the fact that in a race workshop, as machines were broken down and rebuilt, parts would inevitably become mixed. Rhodes remembered:

[Parts] became available to me over a number of years from a variety of sources. And so the project gradually fell into place like a jigsaw. An unusually large barrel and box of forged pistons came with an assortment of parts from up north. The barrel was bigger and longer than anything KTT. With wider spaced stud holes, a double spigot and provision for an oil jet into the cylinder, it proved, along with a couple of long KTT rods found in the West Country, to be from a works engine.[26]

Today the Woods 350cc Velocette – fourth placed in 1937, winner in 1938 and in 1939 – has been lovingly reconstructed by the Rhodes family. It was voted best in show at the Stafford Classic Motorcycle show in April 2002 and now forms part of the displays of Manx National Heritage. It has earned the honour of its accolade as a great TT machine, not only through its association with Woods, but also for the fact that it delivered his tenth and final win, against the looming shadow of war, and against the full weight of the Nazi state.

Chapter 7

500cc Featherbed Norton
(rider Geoff Duke)
1950

Before the Second World War, Norton machinery had dominated motorcycle racing using a frame and engine which remained basically unchanged (apart from minor improvements) for around twenty years, but the increasing speeds and stresses imposed upon their machinery by racing meant that in the postwar years the firm needed to adopt a new style of frame, which was both lightweight and strong. This led to the development of an entirely new Norton racer, which in the hands of an up-and-coming young star named Geoff Duke, would prove to be a formidable motorcycle. The so-called 'featherbed' Norton became a classic machine, indelibly linked to the Isle of Man. This machine, which scored an emphatic victory in the 1950 Senior race, is number seven in our top twenty-five TT machines.

The so-called 'garden gate' Nortons of the 1930s had been incredibly successful in their day, and in the hands of riders such as Harold Daniell had come to dominate the Isle of Man TT. However, by the time racing resumed in the post-Second World War years, increased engine power and rising speeds meant that they had become obsolete, and attempts by Norton engineer Joe Craig to strengthen them had simply made them heavier and harder to handle. An entirely new solution to the problem was needed, and in 1949 Norton were approached by the McCandless brothers, Rex and Cromie, who in their native Northern Ireland had a history of creating innovative frames and other modifications to standard machines. Rex in particular was entirely self-taught as an engineer, stating:

> I never had any formal training. I came to believe that it stops people from thinking for themselves. I read many books on technical subjects, but always regarded that as second-hand knowledge. I did my best working in my own way.[27]

During his early racing career in Northern Ireland, McCandless had experimented with a Triumph, and noticed that removing the front mudguard and headlight, so that there was less weight at the front, improved the handling. He also concluded that a proper suspension system, which enabled the wheels to stay in contact with the road for more of the time, was essential. At this time fast racing motorcycles tended to bounce around a great deal on the road, which was both inefficient in terms of use of power and also produced a lot of unnecessary strain on the working parts. McCandless's early experiments with his Triumph involved taking the suspension dampers from a Citroën car and fitting them to the rear wheel, thus giving it greater road-holding potential. He and his brother had also begun working on ideas for a redesigned frame, and had approached the Triumph firm with them. However, they were rejected by Edward Turner, the autocratic boss of Triumph, and this led them into negotiation with Norton instead. The McCandlesses were convinced that, for all their achievements, Norton did not really understand how racing stresses affected a frame, and what the best ways to compensate for this were.

Craig commissioned them to come up with something new for the company, and the result was an entirely unparalleled frame with a swinging arm, constructed from over forty feet of the best Reynolds tubing. Exceptional lateral rigidity was achieved and in the absence of cast or forged lugs, the weight was also kept down. The two tubes which formed a platform for the fuel tank were a particularly innovative feature. On conventional frames, the fuel tank tended to be draped around a single top tube. The inverted U-shaped recess, which was inevitably necessary in this arrangement, reduced the capacity of the tank as well as making for a weak fitting. In the new Norton arrangement, a reliable tank mounting as well as best use of the space were both achieved. The rear shock absorbers were made by Rex McCandless and had a reservoir built in to stop the oil overheating and cavitating. Rex McCandless held a patent for the design used in 1950, and although Norton would go on to use shock absorbers made by other manufacturers the following year, Geoff Duke later wrote that the McCandless ones were the best he had encountered. McCandless and Artie Bell were responsible for establishing the front fork geometries, angles and off-sets. McCandless fabricated the fork yokes by welding, and modified the fork legs from the 1948 works 'garden gate' model. This geometry was never changed.

Other improvements lay within the engine. Norton had begun working with the British firm of Wellworthy to develop a new form of cylinder. During the war, Wellworthy and its American counterpart the Fairchild Aviation Company had between them developed a cylinder liner which instead of being pressed, shrunk or cast into the finned aluminium jacket, was bonded to the casing by a secret process, which resulted in a 100 per cent heat path. In their product (marketed commercially as 'Al-Fin') the massively improved heat flow increased the cooling capacity in the cylinder jacket, and reduced the tendency towards overheating when an engine was under strain for an extended period, as it was in a race.

Within two months a prototype frame and engine were ready, and were road-tested on the Isle of Man in the winter of 1949. The results were promising, and Norton decided to provide their entire racing team with the new frame for the forthcoming 1950 TT. At that time, the Norton factory was not equipped for bronze welding, and so the McCandless brothers undertook to build all eight frames for the Norton factory riders by hand, using a jig. One of those who tested it was Harold Daniell, who famously declared that it was like lying in a feather bed compared to Norton's earlier frames. The name stuck, and thereafter these machines were known as 'featherbed' or Manx Nortons.

St Helens-born Geoff Duke had honed his skills as a motorcycle dispatch rider in the army during the Second World War, where he had also been part of the Royal Signals White Helmets motorcycle display team. He first competed in the Manx Grand Prix in 1948, and came to the attention of Norton after a good performance in the 1949 meeting. He was soon signed up by the firm. After assisting with testing the new frames, he first rode one in anger at a race meeting at Blandford Camp, Dorset, in April 1950. He won easily. For the 1950 TT he again appeared as a Norton factory rider, his youth and relative inexperience being offset by the fact that some of the Norton mechanics had been with the team since pre-war days, including Ivor Davies and Charlie Edwards, who became Duke's personal mechanic. The Norton garage on the Isle of Man was based at the Manningham Hotel, and it became necessary to place baffles in the exhausts of the machines in order to give the other hotel residents a little more sleep when the bikes were being ridden through the Douglas streets at 5am, on their way to the pits for early morning practice.

Norton's strong performance in the 1950 Junior TT heralded great things for the Senior race, with impressive results in terms of reliability and speed. Now attention was turned to the Senior, and there was much speculation as to whether riders would be forced to conform to team orders – Harold Daniell was the senior Norton rider, but would Duke, the young pretender, be allowed free reign? The Friday of race week in 1950 dawned bright and clear, with weather ideal for racing: warm and dry with just a light breeze. As the ships of the Isle of Man Steam Packet Company drew into Douglas bay early that morning they disgorged some 10,000 additional spectators – the number might have been greater, but a thousand or more were left stranded at Liverpool having missed their connection. Record crowds lined all the vantage points, with a particularly large throng at the Bungalow. The Lieutenant Governor, as always, appeared at the Grandstand half an hour before the beginning of the race.

On the start line, Duke set off as number fifty-seven, facing formidable opposition not only from his experienced Norton teammates, Daniell, Artie Bell and Johnny Lockett, but also from Les Graham on an AJS Porcupine, and Reg Armstrong and Bob Foster on Velocettes. Famously, Geoff was wearing a newly designed set of one-piece leathers, which improved his slipstreaming and reduced air resistance. They were probably worth one or two miles an hour of extra speed and they very quickly caught on with other competitors. Thereafter, one-piece leathers became more or less standard for all riders, whether racing or not. Duke's riding style was distinctive, neat and widely admired, as he was always 'with the bike,' centred in the saddle and with his upper body at the same angle of lean as the machine. For his time, Duke's style was progressive. Before him, many riders leaned the bike, but kept themselves more upright. Stanley Woods described Duke's smooth technique as 'like

Geoff Duke flying down Bray Hill aboard the 'Featherbed' Norton, in the 1950 Senior TT. (Bikesport Fottofinders archives)

water flowing from a tap'. The style really suited the new machine, because in terms of grip and handling the Norton was in a league of its own. From now on, races would not be purely contests of horsepower, they would also be contests of roadholding.

Duke commanded the race almost from the outset, circulating in just over twenty-four minutes on his first lap. Then, on the second circuit, he didn't just break Daniell's 1938 lap record, he utterly obliterated it. Some of the wiser observers commented that it was impossible for a 'novice' like Duke to maintain this kind of pace, and he was bound to either falter or crash, but he did neither. In fact, Duke showed exactly the kind of fearless attitude that would characterise his racing career. He was a man not afraid to take risks, but they were always calculated. He wrote modestly afterwards:

My race was uneventful almost beyond belief. The opening lap of 91.38mph was inside Daniell's 1938 record but did not count, because at that time the starting line was 70 yards further down the road than the line used for timing purposes. However my second lap did the trick at 93.01mph and my lead over Artie, who annexed second place on lap two, increased on each successive lap.

At the refuelling pit stop, I took on the minimum amount of petrol to finish – but this was almost my undoing. My next flying lap was the fifth, which established a lap record of 93.33mph. From then on, I began to change up at lower revs, which probably saved the day for me, because as I rounded the '33rd' for the last time, on the seventh lap, the engine missed a beat. Fuel starvation?

At Governor's Bridge I was on Artie's tail and we crossed the finishing line together. My greatest ambition had been achieved – I had won the Senior TT. When the usual check was made of the first three machines to finish, though, my petrol tank was completely dry![28]

In addition to Duke's natural ability, the new featherbed frame really made the difference, and some spectators noted that the Norton riders were all flowing through the bends so smoothly that it almost seemed like an exhibition race. If the opposition had been faster, then the Nortons might even have pulled more speed out of the bag – it certainly looked to observers on the day that they had the potential. As it was, the main challenger was Les Graham on an AJS, who even though he also broke the existing lap record, only managed fourth place. Norton riders had come home in first, second and third places in the Junior event that week, and that result was the same in the Senior on the Friday. Here Duke claimed first place after having broken both Harold Daniell's

The final McCandless prototype frame moved the petrol tank from its traditional position in front of the seat, and instead stored the fuel in two pannier-style tanks. It thus allowed the rider to get lower behind the slipstreaming, and altered the riding position so much that he now leaned forward while kneeling on the frame. This was too much for the company hierarchy, who could not bring themselves to regard it as a true Norton, and the frame was never adopted. However, sidecar racer Eric Oliver saw it and asked if he could adapt it for sidecar use. It was the beginning of the 'kneeler' style of sidecar outfit that is so familiar today. McCandless, meanwhile, was deeply disillusioned with Norton's conformity and turned his attention to designing cars instead. Nevertheless, the Norton Featherbed became a production motorcycle using Rex McCandless's design and patents, for which in the early years McCandless and his business partner Artie Bell were paid a £1 royalty for each machine sold. Although McCandless had handmade all of the original featherbed frames, on the production machines this was subcontracted to Reynolds Tubing Limited, who continued to make them into the 1970s.

Geoff Duke's 1950 Senior TT-winning machine makes the top twenty-five TT machines in recognition of its association with the legendary rider, but also because of the impact the redesigned frame had on motorcycle development and technology. It marked a clear watershed, a break with the technology of the 1930s, and although it kept Norton competitive for only a few more years, it heavily influenced the design of the Italian machines that began to make a mark in the later 1950s. These in turn influenced Japanese machines, in particular Honda, which would break through in the 1960s.

Duke's actual motorcycle does not survive. The eight 1950 works Nortons were all dismantled at the end of that season, and the parts were used to build the updated 1951 team bikes. Many of the original 1950 parts saw further service in later works bikes, and in many cases were used to destruction. The closest thing to a 1950 works Norton was recently rebuilt by McIntosh Racing in New Zealand, using the only surviving original 1950 works frame. This had been discovered at Beaulieu Autojumble in the 1980s. The owner, Mr Peter Bloore, then embarked on a thirty-year search for original works parts with which to rebuild it. The machine was brought to the Isle of Man in 2015 by Mr Bloore, and exhibited at the Classic TT. In running condition, it completed several laps at Jurby and a lap of the TT course with Bruce Anstey riding, its exhaust filling the air with the authentic roar of a 1950s single-cylinder Norton.

Chapter 8

MV Agusta 500cc (rider John Surtees) 1956

In this chapter, we examine a machine which typifies the Italian domination of the TT, and indeed motorcycle racing as a whole, by the mid-1950s. The multi-cylinder engines developed by the Italian factories had been threatening the supremacy of the single-cylinder engines preferred by the British (particularly Norton) since the start of the decade, but the breakthrough for the Italians had arguably come in 1955, when Geoff Duke, aboard a 500cc Gilera, won the Senior TT, the first time one of their machines had achieved this feat. However the following year the blue riband race on the Island was won by Gilera's great rival MV Agusta, and in the process it brought to prominence one of the greatest motorsport exponents Great Britain has ever produced, a young prodigy named John Surtees. The eighth machine in our line up of TT greats is the motorcycle aboard which Surtees secured this win, on his way to becoming 500cc world champion for the first time.

One of the most stylish of all the Italian motorcycle manufacturers, indeed arguably the most fashionable motorcycle brand in the world, MV Agusta had its roots in the aviation industry. The founder of the company, Count Giovanni Agusta, began building aircraft during the First World War. However, with the post-war slump in orders for planes, the firm was forced to diversify, and began making small inexpensive motorcycles to meet the demand of the Italian domestic market for a cheap form of personal transport. The Second World War hit the company hard and in 1945, as Italy struggled to get back on its feet once more, Giovanni's son, Count Domenico, relaunched the firm as Meccanica Verghera Agusta, again producing small, lightweight motorcycles. The company name was soon shortened simply to MV Agusta.

The early 1950s were a golden age for the Italian motorcycle industry. Racing resumed around this time, and many Italian firms enjoyed enviable reputations for speed and elegance. In particular the racing 125cc two-strokes of MV were a major success story, winning the arduous Milan–Taranto road race in 1950, 1951 and 1952. However, at world championship level the MVs were outclassed by the four-stroke FB-Mondial with its twin-overhead-cam engine. Count Agusta's response to this was to hire rival Italian firm Gilera's chief designer Piero Remor, together with its chief mechanic, Arturo Magni. However, the new Remor-designed 125cc four-stroke was not an immediate success, and it was only following Mondial's withdrawal from racing that MV bagged its first 125cc world championship in 1952. The firm then moved from producing small lightweight machines to larger 500cc models.

MV's 500cc four-cylinder machine first appeared at the Belgian Grand Prix in 1950, with rider Arciso Artesiani finishing fifth. A development of Remor's Gilera design, it followed the same basic layout, but in some respects took a step backwards. The most notable examples of this were the use of only two carburettors and the adoption of shaft drive. The frame and suspension likewise departed from conventional practice, the former consisting of a mixture of tubes and pressings, while the latter featured blade-type girder forks at the front, and a friction-damped 'parallelogram' arrangement at the rear. Gradually these eccentricities were removed, often at the instigation of the team's number one rider, Les Graham. The British ace, a former bomber pilot and holder of the Distinguished Flying Cross, was an immensely talented rider, but his 1951 season was disappointing to say the least.

Misfortune continued to hound the team for the first part of the following season, before Graham scored a breakthrough victory aboard the MV 500 four in the Grand Prix des Nations at Monza, which he followed up by also winning the Spanish Grand Prix. Despite his earlier setbacks, Graham finished second to Gilera's Umberto Masetti in the 1952 world championship. Graham's tragic death at the Isle of Man TT the following year dealt MV's hopes in the 500cc class a devastating blow, and the next few seasons would be relatively lean ones for the team. Only Carlo Ubbiali's victory in the 125cc world championship in 1955 provided a glimmer of satisfaction.

Things began to change for the better in 1956. By this time Remor had departed, leaving Magni in charge of the race team. A 350cc four-cylinder model had been introduced, but it was too big and heavy for its power output, as well as inclined to be temperamental. The 500cc version, however, had gradually been improved upon over the previous few years and now produced a respectable 60bhp at 10,400rpm. By far the most significant development at MV was Domenico Agusta's signing of another British rider, John Surtees, who would reward the Count's faith in his abilities by taking his first 500cc world championship that year. John grew up in a household that was deeply involved in the motorcycle business. His father, Jack Surtees, was a successful motorbike dealer who encouraged his son's emerging interest in the sport, and he began his illustrious career on motorcycles in 1949 as passenger for his father, also a top sidecar racer. As a solo rider he cut his teeth on a Vincent Grey Flash on which he would score his first victory at Brands Hatch in 1951, when he was barely eighteen years of age. He made his first full appearance at the TT in 1954, having sustained an injury in practice the previous year that had put him out of contention.

He later bought a Manx Norton and was invited to join the works team in 1955, clinching his reputation as one of the sport's most gifted rising stars with a memorable victory over Geoff Duke's Gilera at Silverstone at the end of the season. However, he was unable to persuade Norton to continue with a works effort in 1956, despite the firm coming close to attracting commercial sponsorship from a UK national daily paper. In frustration at Norton's apathy, and at Count Domenico's invitation, he switched to the Italian MV Agusta squad for 1956. He then began to ensure that the Surtees name would forever occupy a place in the pages of motorcycle racing history.

Up to this point, the main problem with the 500cc MV machine was not lack of power, but poor handling, largely due to a suspension set-up that was too soft and with too much movement. In 1956, however, everything came together. In terms of the engine, the design of the MV was similar to previous models, with twin overhead camshafts driven by a gear train placed between the inner cylinders. Both cylinders and heads were cast in light alloy, with cast-iron liners. Four Dell'orto carburettors were used to provide the fuel and air mixture; a five-speed gearbox, with a multi-plate clutch, was built into the unit, and a Lucas magneto provided the sparks. However, there was now a major change in the frame and forks. A new tubular duplex cradle-type frame employed swinging-fork rear suspension of conventional type (with chain final drive) and telescopic forks were used at the front. This ironed out the handling problems. The final piece of the jigsaw was Surtees himself. He had proved in the past that he was capable of riding a motorcycle right on the limit of its performance, and this would give MV the edge they needed. Indeed, the rider had a great deal of input into the development of the model into a race-winning machine. He wrote afterwards:

Early in 1956 I went to Italy for several weeks, so that my machines could be adapted to suit my personal requirements. It was a fascinating experience, living in a strange country and working with people who were as unlike my fellow-countrymen as an Esquimaux is as unlike a Tahetian. At first we communicated with each other largely by sign language and scribbled drawings, but I determined to match Arturo [Magni]'s pidgin English with at least a smattering of pidgin Italian, and before long could make myself understood reasonably well. It may seem an unimportant point, but I have always been convinced that my attempt to master their language as soon as possible helped enormously in establishing a friendly understanding with the Italian mechanics.

Before I joined the team, there had been several changes in the frames used for the MV 'fours', and they had tried girder forks and Earles-type pivoted-arm front forks before adopting a fairly conventional telescopic pattern which had the wheel spindle set forward of the centre line, like a Royal Enfield. The frame was tubular, and of the double cradle pattern, and conventional swinging-arm rear forks were employed. The main modifications carried out in that preparatory period were to the suspension units, as I have always attached particular importance to getting the suspension to my liking.[31]

At the 1956 TT, Surtees was leading the Junior race when he ran out of petrol, due to a miscalculation on the part of the mechanics. He stopped on the mountain and borrowed some, and although he finished the race, he was disqualified for refuelling at an unauthorised depot. The Senior would now be his chance to really prove what he could do with MV equipment on the Mountain Course. It was a breezy day, with a strong westerly wind blowing; indeed, some of the gusts approached gale force in exposed places. Travelling marshals reported extremely difficult riding conditions as the wind was strong enough to prevent maximum speed being achieved in some places. No one expected any records to be broken, but the wind also meant that the road surface was dryer than on the two previous race days. There was also some tension in the MV camp. After the refuelling mishap in the Junior race, Surtees wanted his father to handle replenishment when he came into the pits during the Senior. However, he had been over-ruled on this point by team management.

There were other difficulties for Surtees. During practice he had collided with a cow, and in the ensuing tumble grit had been inducted into the engine of his motorcycle. The valve seats had been severely damaged as a result and were beyond local repair. He was now forced to use his second engine, which had already covered many hundreds of miles at other meetings. Although this unit had been stripped and rebuilt in readiness for the Senior, and was perfectly tuned, it was still not the pristine engine on which he had planned to contest the race. One thing had gone to plan, however. The day before the race, at the weigh-in, he had correctly predicted the windy conditions to come and had elected not to use the full 'dustbin' fairing because of the risk of being blown off line.

Surtees, as number 81, was almost the last away at the start of the race, but began in a style that betrayed his short circuit background, roaring away from the line and gaining vital seconds. A four-cylinder machine was easier to start than a single or a twin, but the downside of this was that it also responded to the throttle so fast that it was all too easy to get the front wheel in the air unintentionally, or in wet conditions to spin the back wheel. Surtees had taken time to perfect his starts following an embarrassing incident in his first competitive outing on an MV at Crystal Palace, when he started so rapidly that he spent the first few hundred yards riding side-saddle with his front wheel in the air!

On the first lap of the 1956 Senior, local rider Derek Ennett was leading the field at Ballacraine, but Surtees was flying and came into Braddan Bridge much too fast, forcing him to brake heavily and to take a rather unorthodox line. Despite having set off as number 81, in the first twenty-four miles he overtook a dozen or more riders. By the end of lap one, his time showed that he was leading the race – a position he did not relinquish. However, as he

John Surtees in winning form aboard the MV Agusta in the 1956 Senior TT. This photograph shows the machine without the full fairing, which was dispensed with by Surtees because of the windy conditions. (Manx National Heritage)

came past the pits at the end of the first lap he gave what appeared to be a thumbs down signal, while pointing to the rear wheel. It later transpired that the combination of full tank and high winds had made the rear wheel lose grip when the rider braked and the fuel surged forward. The signal was to warn the pit crew to ready the the spare suspension legs, as he initially thought that one or other on the machine had failed, but the problem soon cured itself.

The pace took its toll on other riders, with numerous retirements, including Bob McIntyre, on the second lap. By the third lap, Surtees had fought his way through the field and was eleventh on the road. He stopped for fuel and this time there was no mistake: the tank was brimmed full before he set off again. Bill Lomas and John Hartle continued to press him right to the end of the race, but even though the former had elected to carry enough fuel on his Moto Guzzi not to have to come in for more, he was still half a minute down on Surtees after his stop. As it was, so commanding was Surtees's lead, that by the final lap it was taken by the spectators as a foregone conclusion that he would win, and attention switched momentarily to the battle for second and third places between Hartle and Lomas. Surtees crossed the line to great applause from the chilled spectators in the grandstand, and handed MV their first 500cc success at the Isle of Man TT.

In reflecting on the race a few days afterwards, Surtees commented that while the Norton was capable of incredible things in terms of handling, the Agusta was a very different proposition. At speeds of over 100mph, conscious physical effort was required to guide it through swerves such as those at Quarry Bends on the Isle of Man, and sudden changes of direction were extremely difficult to execute. He speculated that had he been forced to do so, he could have gone even faster, but on a course that he was still learning, with a machine that was still unfamiliar, he would not have wanted to. However, his success at only his third TT suggested he had great ability, not least in learning the course. Surtees reflected afterwards:

> I think I shall always look upon the TT races of 1956 as my starting point on the road to the World Championship... This success gave me a great fillip. I had notched up my first points towards [it] and it was on this that I concentrated in the following weeks.[32]

Surtees posted impressive wins at the Dutch TT and Belgian Grand Prix, and despite a bad crash at Solitude in Germany later in the season, which put him in hospital for several weeks, his win in the Senior TT set him on course to take the 500cc world title in 1956, an outstanding achievement for the twenty-two-year-old. It would be a cause of great regret to him that MV's main rivals, Gilera and Moto Guzzi, soon withdrew from Grand Prix racing, leaving the MV squad to dominate the scene. Even so, Surtees's performances were still remarkable. In the three seasons up to the end of 1960, when he left professional motorcycle racing for good, John won the 350cc and 500cc world championships, as well as the Senior and Junior Isle of Man TT in 1958 and 1959, plus the Senior once again in 1960. Yet he was always disappointed that the autocratic Count Domenico Agusta proved increasingly reluctant to field motorbikes in non-championship and British domestic events, or even to permit Surtees to use his own private Nortons in these meetings.

This lack of flexibility on Agusta's part led Surtees to take the initiative to supplement his racing programme. The Count may have been contractually able to restrict John's motorcycle racing, but there was nothing to prevent him competing on four wheels. Surtees was effectively given little choice but to turn his back on motorcycle competition and go into car racing. As a driver

The 1956 specification machine, rebuilt by John Surtees, in the Barber Motorsports Museum, Leeds, Alabama, where it now resides. (Author's collection)

he was equally successful, becoming the only man ever to win a world title on two wheels and on four, and he later became a team owner, becoming a friend and mentor to Mike Hailwood when he took a similar career path.

The 1956 500cc MV was an important machine in TT history for a number of reasons. It gave Surtees the first of his six TT wins, and it gave MV their first Senior win on the Mountain Course, and in spite of Giacomo Agostini's extensive use of MV machinery at the TT in the late 1960s and early 1970s, this was arguably the firm's most significant single achievement on the Isle of Man. Sadly, relatively little of MV's racing heritage is now held by the company itself. When the Italian government stepped in to take control of the company following economic difficulties, the contents of the MV race shop were sold off following a lengthy period in storage. At this time only two machines of the pre-1965 period were assembled and complete, the remainder being dismantled. Following this sale, the principal owners of MV's racing heritage were Robert Iannucci in the USA, Ubaldo Elli in Italy and John Surtees in the UK. Surtees, with the help of former head mechanic Arturo Magni, was able to obtain sufficient parts to reassemble a machine of the same specification as the 1956 Senior TT winner. This machine, which undoubtedly does contain some of the parts from the actual winning motorcycle, was owned by Surtees until 1993. Since then this MV Agusta, which is the closest we may ever be able to get to the historic 1956 winner, has been held by the Barber Vintage Motorsports Museum in Leeds, Alabama. It is usually on display, but has been paraded on a number of occasions, most notably when it was awarded first place in its class at the Concours d'Elegance at Pebble Beach in 2011.

Chapter 9

500cc Gilera (rider Bob McIntyre) 1957

A piece of genuine TT history was made during the Senior race in 1957, when 100mph lap barrier was broken for the first time. This milestone, which had been the subject of much speculation, and which controversially had first been awarded to Geoff Duke in 1955 before being withdrawn, was finally reached by Bob McIntyre, the so-called 'flying Scotsman'. McIntyre achieved the feat aboard an Italian Gilera machine, having been recommended to the factory by Duke, their regular rider, who was injured. The magnificent and iconic four-cylinder 500cc Gilera, with its distinctive engine note, is the subject of this chapter.

Gilera's history of racing four-cylinder motorcycles goes all the way back to 1936, when the factory bought the rights to the CNA 'Rondine' machine, which utilised this arrangement. The Rondine was the first practical bike to have the cylinders transposed across the frame in the manner which, much later, the Japanese would make the industry standard. At the time, British factories still believed that a single-cylinder engine was the best design for racing, and that remained the case with most of the British manufacturers until, by the early 1960s, it was obvious they were uncompetitive.

The Gilera company was owned, and tightly controlled, by founder Count Giuseppe Gilera, who had ambitions to make his firm a world leader in motorcycle design and production. As well as being an astute businessman Gilera was a talented motorcycle racer and mechanic, and understood the potential of the four-cylinder engine – as well as the publicity it could bring to the Arcore factory. His first big breakthrough came at the 1950 Belgian Grand Prix when Umberto Masetti took victory on one of his four-cylinder machines. Always retaining an across the frame design for cooling purposes, the Gilera 'Four' could be troublesome and underwent many redesigns before it reached its ultimate form. This was the five-speed 1957 design, which gave Bob McIntyre the Senior TT, and his team mate Libero Liberati the 500cc world championship.

The motor was still a two-valve-per-cylinder design, but the highly talented and practical Franco Passoni had increased the cylinder bore to 58.8mm with two pairs of cylinder heads. There were four separate cylinder barrels and one long magnesium cam cover – and the whole lot was bolted to the crankcases via twelve long studs. The valves were opened by a gear train, because this was considered to be the most reliable method available at the time. Gears were also used for the primary drive to the clutch, again for reliability, and they fed the power to a five-speed gearbox with the classic right-hand side European gear shift pattern of 'one up and four down.' A one-gallon oil sump was positioned beneath the engine, to help to lower the centre of gravity.

In this trim, the motor produced around 70hp and the bike weighed 150kg (330lb). This was some 18kg (40lb) heavier than the best Manx Norton or Matchless G50s – but with an impressive 20hp more than the British singles. A top-quality Manx Norton was at this time capable of around 135mph – and that was a really world-class example – in contrast with the Gilera which would, in the right conditions, be touching 155mph. Far more importantly, in terms of acceleration the Gilera could simply leave a Manx or G50 standing. With its two-valve cylinder heads, 100 degree valve angle and steeply domed pistons, the engine was a classic piece of 1950s technology, and (perhaps fairly) some people at the time believed that the design, after many years of development, had reached the limit of its performance.

Nonetheless, speed and acceleration were not everything. The early Gileras were notoriously difficult to ride, and when Geoff Duke eventually left Norton to join the Italian firm, he brought with him an intimate knowledge of the best handling race bike in the world at the time: the Norton 30M Manx. Geoff made a number of suggestions to the development engineer, Piero Taruffi, intended to bring the Gilera closer to the Norton in terms of handling performance. Taruffi and Duke got on well and the former took on board the English rider's advice. Subsequently a new shorter frame, which lowered the engine, became the Gilera standard. This resulted in a stretched out riding position, very similar to that on the Norton. The effect on the handling of the machine was dramatic, and combined with the powerful engine made it one of the best in the world. As for brakes, the Gilera was equipped with a formidable 220mm double-sided four-leading-shoe front brake, and a single-sided twin-leading-shoe rear brake. Contrary to popular belief, drum brakes can in fact provide enormous braking power when compared to a disc brake system. The problems are that they are much more complex to make, much more difficult to use, and fade under severe use. In the case of the Gilera front brake, it had a ferocious self-servo effect. Once the brake shoes bit, the rider had to ease the lever pressure in order to prevent the front wheel from locking uncontrollably, often with disastrous results. Modern tyres would offset this effect considerably, by providing more grip and therefore more friction with the road, but in 1957 it would have a taken a highly skilled rider to prevent the wheel from locking. The overall appearance of the machine was finished off by a classic 'dustbin' fairing that covered the entire front wheel and engine: the big Gilera four was known to many in the 1950s as the 'fire engine' because of its bright red livery.

This powerful and attractive machine was, due to Duke's injury, now in the hands of one of the most capable riders of his day. Bob McIntyre was twenty-nine years old and from Scotstoun in Glasgow. He had started his working life in the city's shipyards before moving to Cooper Brothers motorcycle dealers in Troon, who were also his first sponsors. McIntyre had a great affinity for mechanics and did much of the tuning work on his own machines. Later he teamed up with former racer Joe Potts, who supplied him with Norton machinery. He had had only a few outings on Gilera motorcycles before the 1957 TT, but he rewarded the Italian factory's faith in him by winning the Junior event aboard their 350cc machine early in race week, setting a record speed for that class in the process. TT week of 1957 had enjoyed more than the usual carnival atmosphere, as it was the Golden Jubilee of the meeting. The Thursday night before the Senior race was calm and clear, and it was estimated that an extra 17,000 people travelled to the Island that day to watch the race and join the many thousands of spectators who were already present. The Friday of race week was the culmination of the celebrations and the programme opened at 10am with a parade from Creg-ny-Baa to the grandstand, featuring many past TT winners and an array of vintage machines.

After this the Senior TT got underway, run over eight laps instead of the usual seven in celebration of the Jubilee (an unusual decision on the part of the ACU organisers, who, as it was noted at the time, had paid no attention to the feelings or discomfort of the riders when setting the greater distance). Unlike the other factory Gilera in the race, which carried all its fuel high up in a seven-gallon tank, McIntyre's machine featured a smaller top tank and two pannier tanks within the fairing. This reduced the centre of gravity, and made his machine much easier to handle. He went out as number 78, the number also stitched into the back panel of his black leathers, as was the norm at the time.

The only incident that troubled McIntyre during the race was when he was struck hard on the forehead by a stone thrown up by the rear wheel of another motorcycle, while exiting Union Mills on the fifth lap. The injury is

This illustration of Bob McIntyre at the 1957 TT shows the bright red and white fairing of the Gilera, giving rise to the nickname 'fire engine'. (Courtesy of Peter Haynes)

clearly apparent in photographs of McIntyre taken immediately afterwards. In writing about the race, McIntyre recalled:

> [as] I accelerated away, a stone hit me, thrown up by the wheels of another rider I was about to lap. It was probably no bigger than a pea, but at 100mph it felt like a brick. It caught me between my goggles and my crash helmet and cut my left temple. I felt dazed and sick, it brought tears to my eyes and I felt blood running. But fortunately, the rush of cold air coagulated the blood above my goggles.[33]

Despite the fact that it had just completed nearly 302 miles of racing, when McIntyre's machine went into technical inspection after he crossed the finishing line, it proved to be in remarkable condition. All the combustion chambers appeared in good order with no sign of undue heat. The rear tyre was little more than half worn, while front tyre wear was even less. There was a small amount of oil on the rear wheel rim, and the chain was taut and not in need of adjustment. McIntyre joined a select band of only five other men who had achieved a Junior/Senior double at the TT, and broke the 100mph barrier four times during the race, achieving 101.03mph on his second lap, 100.54 on his third, 101.12 on his fourth lap and 100.35 on his sixth lap. His average speed over the eight laps was also a record at 98.99 mph.

Amazingly, despite all their efforts at development, the success they had already achieved and the potential that lay ahead, 1957 was to be the last year of competition for Gilera, apart from a brief flirtation with racing in the mid-1960s. Perhaps it was true that the engine had reached the limit of its development, and only the difficult task of totally redesigning it would keep the firm successful. If so, this was probably a factor in their decision to withdraw from Grand Prix racing at the end of the season, citing economic

Bob McIntyre is congratulated by John Surtees after winning the 1957 Senior TT. The cut from a stone is clearly visible above McIntyre's left eye. (Bikesport Fottofinders archives)

reasons, along with Moto Guzzi and FB Mondial. Although a Gilera factory museum does exist, in the form of the Museo Piaggio at Pontedera, fifteen minutes' drive east of Pisa, McIntyre's TT-winning machine is not there. The 1957 racing machines were used at Monza at the end of the year in a series of world speed record attempts. After that, their fate becomes rather obscure, though it is reported that in 1959 Geoff Duke visited the Gilera factory to try to persuade Giuseppe Gilera to take the old racing machines out of mothballs and allow McIntyre to use them as a privateer during the 1960 season. The count turned down this request.

With the withdrawal of the Italian teams, McIntyre was left without a racing contract and returned to campaigning Nortons. He had briefly flirted with Honda, but found the terms of their contract too restrictive. By 1961, however, matters had been resolved and he entered the 250cc race at that year's TT on a Honda. Geoff Duke meanwhile was still pursuing Gilera, and briefly it looked as though his determination had paid off – the count agreed to release the 500cc bike from 1957. However, when he found out that McIntyre had agreed to ride for Honda in the smaller classes the offer was abruptly withdrawn. By 1963 Duke had formed his own team, Scuderia Duke, and with Phil Read and John Hartle signed up as riders he at last managed to persuade the company hierarchy in Arcore to lend him three of the 1957 machines to campaign in the 500cc and 350cc world championships. However, in the six years that Gilera had been out of top-flight racing there had been no development work done, and the team's results served only to underline how far their rivals had advanced. In the 1963 Senior TT, Read managed third place and Hartle second behind Mike Hailwood's MV Agusta, while in the smaller class Honda was dominant. Scuderia Duke was wound up the following year, the Gilera machines went back into mothballs, and their eventual fate remains shrouded in mystery. If the Gilera museum had owned the 1957 Senior TT-winning machine, then it would presumably be a star exhibit, but the displays consist mainly of examples of over-the counter models. All that can be said with certainty is that in 2017 one of the 1957 500cc machines, with frame number 15 and engine number 15, was offered for sale by Sotheby's RM Auctions in Italy. The sale catalogue noted that the machine had been one of those loaned to Scuderia Duke, after which it was owned for a time by Piero Lardi, before being sold into the collection of Arigo Manar and Vittorio Martello in 1982. Used in 2000 by Sante Trioschi, the bike was most recently run in 2014, at a classic meeting at the Paul Ricard circuit in France. This may well be the machine used by Bob McIntyre to break the magical 100mph barrier at the TT.

As for the man himself, in 1962 McIntyre began looking into the possibility of racing cars, and he consulted Formula 1 driver and fellow Scot Jackie Stewart on this point. He even went as far as arranging a successful test drive at Goodwood. However, when the season started he was still very much involved in racing motorcycles, and he died after an accident in a wet race at Oulton Park in Cheshire. His name, and the name of Gilera, will forever be associated with the Isle of Man TT. The pairing achieved the iconic first 100mph lap, so the machine secures its place in the top twenty-five greatest machines in the history of the event.

Chapter 10

125cc Honda
(rider Mike Hailwood)
1961

The story of Honda's arrival at the TT is the stuff of legend, but it bears retelling here. Soichiro Honda, the visionary founder of the Japanese motor company, had set his sights on breaking into the European motorcycle market, and reasoned that the best way to prove his machines was through racing success at the Isle of Man TT. Amazingly it took him only four years to turn that ambition into reality. The tenth machine in our run down of the top twenty-five is doubly important in the history of the TT, for not only did it mark Honda's first win on the Isle of Man, and the beginning of its rise to become a global supercompany, but it was also the first victory of an up-and-coming young star named Mike Hailwood.

Soichiro Honda had been a motorcar racer in his native Japan in the 1930s, but he was also an astute and innovative businessman. He founded a number of companies during his lifetime, but as he later freely admitted, not all of them were successful. During the Second World War he ran a firm producing piston rings for aircraft engines, but following the defeat of Japan he sold the business. In 1948 he started a new venture fitting war surplus engines into bicycle frames, and called it the Honda Motor Company.

Japanese goods had a poor reputation in the 1950s, and were often viewed as inferior copies of western products. Indeed, it is fair to say that in the immediate post-war years Honda's machines were not spectacular. However, Honda needed to overcome negative perceptions and the best way to do that would be to prove the quality of his products in the toughest environment of all. He came to the Isle of Man TT – the pinnacle of motorcycle racing – in 1957, and vowed that the next year a Honda team would be back and that they would win. In fact it was 1959 before a Honda factory team made it to the Island. All of their riders at that time were inexperienced in racing on the Isle of Man. Although they carried off the team prize that year (a creditable achievement), Soichiro Honda himself recognised that there was still some way to go, both in terms of machinery and riders, before they would achieve individual success.

He knew he could improve on the speed and performance of his bikes through hard work, but recognised that Honda would also need to recruit western riders with TT experience if they were to gain podium places. One of these riders was the young Mike Hailwood, aged just twenty-one when he came to the 1961 TT. Although he was young, he was far from inexperienced. Hailwood was seventeen when he began motorcycle racing and his millionaire father Stan, the owner of King's of Oxford, paid for him to go to South Africa to practice and hone his skills under the tuition of more experienced riders. He rode in his first TT in 1958, and three years later had seen the way in which Honda machinery was developing as well as its potential.

It was as a privateer in his father's Ecurie Sportive team that Hailwood entered his 125cc Honda in the Ultra Lightweight race that year, although he did receive some factory assistance. Honda differed from other manufacturers because the racing bikes they supplied to privateers and satellite teams were every bit as good as those used by their own factory team. Honda believed that a win was a win, whoever rode the bike, so long as it had Honda's name on the side. However, Hailwood was almost a non-starter because the bike his father had ordered from Honda hadn't turned up. Mike himself was quite resigned to the fact, but his father was more determined, and pestered the Honda team constantly. Stan said:

> Honda had promised Mike both a 125 and a 250, but there was a shortage of 125s and not until the final practice session, after persistent worrying, did we get a 125. I practically lived at the Honda camp that day and in the end, just to get rid of me I think, they said: 'All we have is Taveri's practice machine'. They told me it was a bit worse for wear but I could take it. Naturally I grabbed it and had it back at our camp before they could change their minds. We looked it over and Mike took it up the road. His remarks are perhaps, better left unsaid. In short, it was 'clapped out'. However we decided he should do one lap very gently to get used to it and comply with the regulations. He came in and told me he was staggered by the performance and only wished it was in better shape. We went over everything, checking nuts, bolts, etc but without much hope of it lasting the course.[34]

Mike later recalled that his mechanics tightened up just about anything they could lay a spanner on as they prepared the machine, and this did have the effect of smoothing it out a little. Even so, he and his father had little confidence that the 125 would go the distance. The Ultra Lightweight 125cc race was scheduled for Monday 12 June 1961, with Honda factory rider Jim Redman leading the field away. After half a lap, Taveri and Hailwood had caught Redman, passing him before the Guthrie memorial. As the two diced for first place, Hailwood broke the lap record by two miles an hour. This incredibly exciting event was captured on one of the earliest pieces of colour film shot at the TT, with commentary by Graham Walker, who utters the memorable line, 'its Honda, Honda, Honda all the way' as the top three positions were held by the trio of Taveri, Hailwood and Tom Phillis, all jostling for position. Stan continued:

> It was agreed that Mike should go flat out until it packed up. We were staggered when, on the first lap, he caught Honda's lightweight star Luigi Taveri, who had started ten seconds earlier, to smash the lap record from a standing start. On the second lap he broke it again, setting a new record, and increasing his lead over Taveri. Came the last lap and going up the Mountain the expected happened. The edge went off the motor and Taveri, two stones lighter, began catching up. Mike went berserk on corners trying to keep up but Luigi pulled away on the straights. We were sweating in the pits as Taveri came in first, and counting the seconds for Mike to arrive. He only just managed to win... A close shave![35]

Not only was this Mike's first-ever TT win, but it was also the first for Honda. The machine on which he won was designated as a 2RC143 by the factory that built it. It was an improvement on the previous year's RC143, and this in turn was an improvement on the preceding RC142. In contrast to the RC142, the air-cooled, four-stroke, twin-cylinder engine of the RC143 was canted forward by thirty-five degrees to improve cooling and increase air flow to the newly designed Keihin carburettors. The engine featured double overhead camshafts, driven by a vertical shaft through bevel gears. The engine was said to produce 22hp (16kW) at 14,000rpm. The leading link front forks, which had proved successful on Japanese dirt tracks, had been identified as a particular weakness on tarmac and were replaced by more conventional telescopic forks for the Isle of Man. This change to the forks, along with the change to the engine design, helped move the centre of gravity of the bike much further forward. The open-cradle frame was also considerably strengthened compared to the previous year's model.

The 1961 2RC143 makes the top twenty-five TT machines by virtue of the fact that it gave both Honda and Hailwood their first win on the Isle of Man. At the time, Hailwood was still a novice, so all of the media attention

Mike Hailwood after his first TT victory. It was also a historic moment for Honda, giving them their first TT win. (Bikesport Fottofinders archives)

was focussed upon Honda. It is only in retrospect that we see it as the first in a phenomenal series of wins by the legendary 'Mike the Bike'. It was also indicative of the strength of Honda technology that a machine that had taken such a battering during practice could subsequently turn in a race-winning performance. It is no exaggeration to say that this event, followed of course by the emergence of Suzuki, Yamaha and Kawasaki, signalled the end of the British motorcycle industry, which had been too complacent in the face of growing foreign competition. Prophetically, one British newspaper ran a story in the wake of the 1961 Honda victories which stated:

The Rising Sun of Japan blazed brightly over the TT races at the Isle of Man last week, as Japanese motorcycles won the first five places in both the 125cc and 250cc events. How did the Japanese manufacturers – whose machines were competing at the Isle of Man for only the third time – achieve their spectacular success? To find the answer, a British motorcycle firm stripped down one of the Japanese machines. What they discovered spells a grim warning to Britain's motorcycle exporters. This is what the British firm's works director said: 'When we stripped the machine, frankly, it was so good it frightened us. It was made like a watch and it wasn't a copy of anything. It was the product of original thinking and very good thinking.'[36]

There is doubt about what became of the motorcycle Mike rode that day in 1961. Some believe that the bike was subsequently presented 'to the people of the Isle of Man' by Soichiro Honda, in grateful recognition of the part the Island had played in securing the future of his company, and that it resided for many years in the private Murray Motorcycle Museum on the Island. In the early 2000s the owner downsized and sold the machine back to the Honda corporation. The Murray Museum website now states:

> One of the motorcycles that proved to be the most sought after, on display and for sale, was a Honda works 125cc twin cylinder, the racer from 1961. This was the bike that was given to Charlie [Murray] for [sic] Mr Honda's private collection. In the mid-70's, Mr Honda was on a world tour and made a visit to 'Murray's', whilst on the Isle of Man. Charlie asked Mr Honda through an interpreter, if it would be possible to have a Honda race motorcycle for the museum. When he returned home to Japan, he sent the 125cc racer as a gift. During the sale [of] the motorcycles in 2006, Peter [Murray] got in touch with Honda, and they informed him that they would like to 'buy' back the bike, so a price was agreed on and the bike went back to Honda Japan. As this motorcycle had come from Mr Honda's private collection, Honda were keen to have it back whatever the cost. The motorcycle was probably the race bike Kunimitsu Takahashi rode when he won the 1961 Ulster Grand Prix, and not the bike that Mike Hailwood rode when he won the 1961 TT.[37]

Be that as it may, the Honda company apparently believed it to be the Hailwood machine, and it now resides in the Honda Collection Hall at Hamamatsu, unequivocally labelled as the first Honda winner at the Isle of Man TT, ridden by Mike Hailwood. One other intriguing snippet of information also offers a clue as to the real fate of the Hailwood machine. Ted Macauley, Mike's friend and biographer, states in the book *Hailwood* that Honda had agreed to supply Stan with a 125 and a 250 machine for the 1961 TT. Macauley further adds that the firm's gratitude for winning their first TT did not intrude into business

The 1961 125cc-winning machine, ridden by Mike Hailwood and now in the Honda Collection Hall. (Author's collection)

matters and they still billed Stan for £200 for the *shipping* of two machines from Japan (not for their purchase). This suggests that the machines were only on loan, a situation confirmed by the fact that Mike then states that through a fiddle his father managed to hang on to the 250 machine, whereas letting the 125 go was no great loss, because he had decided to give up racing in that class. This does imply that the 125 machine was returned to Honda, which further supports the theory that this was the true identity of the machine in the Murray museum.

In any event, the machine that gave both Mike Hailwood and Honda their first TT wins was a truly special object. It created two giants of the racing and automotive world, one of which, Honda, became one of the most significant motor companies in existence today, and the other, Mike Hailwood, who became a legend to generations of racing fans for his exploits on four wheels as well as two. It is hard to overstate Mike Hailwood's importance to the TT, but some idea of his significance in relation to the event comes from the fact that this motorcycle is the first of three amazing machines associated with Mike that feature in this book.

Chapter 11

500cc BMW sidecar outfit (riders Klaus Enders/Ralf Englehardt) 1973

Given the dominance of German machinery in the sidecar classes at the TT in the 1960s and early 1970s, one of these three-wheeler outfits was bound to make the top twenty-five. But which one? During these years, the 500cc sidecar race at the Isle of Man TT was also the British round of the sidecar world championship, so the events were closely linked, with success in one vital to the other. Two notable German sidecar outfits sold at auction by Bonhams in recent years have been the Helmut Fath URS combination, which was a TT competitor and world championship-winner in 1969 and 1972, and Georg Auerbacher's BMW-engined machine, which competed at the TT and other events in the late 1960s. However, although both outfits are impressive, and won numerous grands prix, neither of them could honestly be described as a really outstanding TT machine. From a TT perspective, the greatest German sidecar outfit of this era is probably that ridden to two TT wins in 1973 by Klaus Enders. Not only was it a highly successful TT competitor, but it was also a world-class Grand Prix outfit, and its association with Enders, the most successful German motorcycle racer ever, makes it truly special. This chapter explores its history.

The origin of the 1973 Enders machine is interesting. Sidecar racing in general had a special place in West Germany in the post-war decades, which stemmed from the huge part that motorcycles and sidecars had played in that country as a cheap means of private transport. For almost two decades, from 1954 to 1974, the Munich firm of Bayerische Motoren Werke AG (BMW) had a stranglehold over the sidecar world championship. Only in two seasons, 1968 (Fath and Kalauch) and 1971 (Owesle and Rutherford), was the title captured from them, and on both occasions it was by the same immensely powerful URS outfit mentioned above. URS was Fath's own make, the engine being developed entirely by him in response to his rejection by BMW, whose equipment he had previously ridden. Sensing the threat that the homemade

URS represented, for the 1972 season the Munich manufacturer was eager to bring the world championship title back to Bavaria. For this purpose the factory promised extensive support to the already successful Grand Prix trio of Klaus Enders (driver), Ralf Englehardt (passenger) and Dieter Busch (sponsor, constructor and engine tuner). The trio already had a record of success, having been world champions in three times.

Klaus Enders, born in 1937 in Wetzlar, about forty miles north of Frankfurt, started his racing career in the early 1960s. Initially he had competed as a solo rider and sidecar driver simultaneously, and in 1963 he won the 500cc German junior solo championship, followed in 1964 by the overall German 500cc championship. However, the cost of competing across the board forced him to make a decision, and in 1966 he chose to focus on sidecar racing. His first sidecar world championship came in 1967, with a second title in 1969 and a third in 1970. For the 1971 season, Enders withdrew from sidecar competition to try to break into four-wheeled racing, but was unsuccessful. In 1972, following the humiliation of BMW in the sidecar world championship, he took up the Bavarian firm's offer of support, and with Dieter Busch began to develop a machine capable of retaking the sidecar world title. Busch reached deep into his bag of tricks, and built a delicate one-piece monocoque chassis using aircraft steel only one millimetre thick. From the standard BMW 500cc flat twin Rennsport engine he also developed a powerplant with an additional third bearing at the centre, and its own ignition system. This motor, when tuned, produced 67hp. The wheels and brake system were developed in parallel, in the workshop of Klaus Enders. Because he thought very little of disc brakes, Enders favoured a double-duplex drum brake system, and constructed his own hubs for the wheels. Due to the fact that BMW's commitment to support them had come quite late in the day, it was not until the third world championship race of the season, at the Salzburgring on 14 May, that they were ready to compete. They had already missed the West German and French rounds, which went to Siegfried Schauzu and Heinz Luthringhauser respectively. However, it had been worth the wait, for Enders and Englehardt took victory in that first outing in Austria.

The next meeting was the Isle of Man TT. Here Enders and Englehardt were less successful, retiring in both the 500cc and 750cc races, but they went on to take three more victories with wins at the Dutch TT at Assen, the Belgian round at Spa and the Czechoslovakian Grand Prix at Brno. With seventy-two points, and a nine-point lead over nearest rival Luthringhauser, it was enough to give them the world title. Using the same outfit they went into the 1973 season as reigning world champions. This was to be a historic season in Grand Prix terms, for out of seven starts, Enders and Englehardt won them all, giving them their fifth world title and BMW their eighteenth. They came to the Isle of Man TT as favourites, and threw down the gauntlet when in practice they unofficially broke the lap record. The first sidecar outing of the meeting was the 750cc race on the Saturday and conditions were less than ideal. A still-wet road was slowly drying under a clearing sky and with a warm breeze, and the packed field was thinned by a number of machines that flatly refused to fire up. As the race got underway, Siegfried Schauzu (or 'Sideways Sid' as he was affectionately known to British fans) intended to show Enders that he would not be having things all his own way. Schauzu, who was also BMW-powered, actually caught him at the Bungalow, and kept the pressure on right through those first two laps. The roadsides were littered with British riders whose outfits had failed, but the two Teutonic knights jostled for position, urged on by shouts of 'schnell, schnell' from the many German spectators who lined the course. By the third lap it was noticeable that Schauzu's pace was slowing and Enders was able to draw away from him. Indeed, he was on blistering form and took the chequered flag with over a minute to spare. It was an incredible performance with a new lap record and a new race time and race speed being set.

Klaus Enders and Ralf Engelhardt coming out of Ramsey in the 1973 750cc sidecar TT. Note the damage to the front of the outfit from loose stone chips. (Bikesport Fottofinders archives)

Even greater things were to follow on Monday 4 June 1973, when the 500cc event, the one that counted for world championship points, was run. For the fans soaking up the sun on the banks and hedges as they waited for the race to start, there was only one possible outcome. Enders was the clear favourite to win. Only one man had done the sidecar 'double' up to this point, his rival Siegfried Schauzu. Schauzu was under no illusions about how far out of contention he was, telling reporters: 'Enders is too fast for me. I know. So I plan to go for second place.'[38]

The weather was ideal with a dry road and a gentle breeze blowing. For Enders and Englehardt, however, it was a bad start, for it took them thirty yards of hard pushing to get the outfit to fire up. Nevertheless, Enders quickly started carving his way through the eight competitors on the road ahead of him, bypassing Schauzu as he did so, and by Ballacraine was he was in the lead on time. By Ballaugh it was thought that he might well be on course for the first 100mph sidecar lap. Rocketing through Ramsey, he was leading on the road as well as time by the time he reached the Bungalow, and held an incredible forty-eight-second lead over second-place man Schauzu. With Brits cast aside once more, by this stage in the race German machines were in first, second, third and fourth places. The real battle was between BMW and its rival König, as Rolf Steinhausen tried to get in on the action. The first lap was a new record set by Enders, and he powered through the second in fine style. Schauzu was by now one minute forty seconds astern, and nothing short of a major misfortune to Enders would hand him the race. By the third lap, engine preservation was becoming Enders's main concern, but even so he set another lap record on his final circuit. The *TT Special* noted:

> Last lap excitement continued with Enders heading for his first double TT victory and more World Championship points. Everywhere he gets the acclaim of the spectators. This acclaim is more than well deserved for he is on the peak of his skill and he is a delight to watch. With 45 World Championship points already in the bag another 15 look like putting him in an unassailable position for the world crown.[39]

As the German national anthem drifted across the grandstand and paddock following the garlanding ceremony, the sun was setting on one of the finest days of racing in the long history of the TT, a glorious day for German motorsport, and certainly one of the best days in the annals of sidecar racing on the Isle of Man.

In 1974 the BMW factory retired from sidecar Grand Prix racing, so Enders and Englehardt competed using the same machine but under the HBM banner.

Enders (right) and Engelhardt show reporters their battle-scarred helmets following victory in the 1973 750cc sidecar race. (Bikesport Fottofinders archives)

The abbreviation represented the name of their main sponsor, the Frankfurt BMW dealer Gert Heukerott, HBM standing for 'Heukerott Busch Motor'. Again in 1974, despite reduced BMW support and the growing threat from Berlin-based factory König, whose machinery was growing in popularity, they again took the world title, only two points ahead of runners-up Schwärzel and Kleis on a two-stroke König. It was the swansong for the BMW flat twin engine, for at the TT and elsewhere it would be briefly eclipsed by the König, before Yamaha TZ engines swept all before them in the sidecar field.

After that final world championship, Enders never raced again (despite numerous offers) and became a successful businessman in the precision engineering industry, making parts for dentistry and also for golf buggies and the automotive market. He retired from his business in 2003, preferring to spend his time with his wife on the golf course near their home in Asslar-Werdorf. With six world championships to their names, Enders and Englehardt are the second most successful motorsport competitors in German history – only Formula 1 star Michael Schumacher has had more success.

For many years the Enders machine was in the hands of German sidecar racer and enthusiast Heinz Bals. As a cultural icon and the only surviving BMW championship-winning machine, it has a special place in German motorsport history. In 2004–05 it received an overhaul from BMW technicians, and the engine was found to be in incredibly good condition. The only other major alteration Bals undertook was to return the outfit to its 1973 colour scheme. As a general rule of thumb, historic racing cars or motorcycles are only really interesting to many enthusiasts when they are in roadworthy condition. The engine must be running faultlessly, and they should ideally be used for racing on certain occasions, or for demonstration laps of honour. This, however, places these iconic machines at risk of serious mishap. Unusually, Bals took a more enlightened view than most enthusiasts, saying:

> For my Enders sidecar I have categorically rejected this idea. The world championship sidecar was too valuable for veterans races and the risk that something would break was just too big. Especially when you consider that just this original winning outfit is left out of 19 BMW world champion titles.[40]

It is now believed that the Enders outfit is with a collector in Japan, Bals having sold it for an undisclosed six-figure sum, though its exact location is uncertain. Nevertheless, as one of the most successful German sidecar outfits of the 1960s and 1970s, a multiple TT-winner and multiple world championship-winner, as well as arguably the greatest BMW-engined outfit in an era dominated by the Munich manufacturer, the Enders outfit carves a niche for itself in the TT's twenty-five greatest-ever machines.

Chapter 12

750cc Triumph T150 'Slippery Sam' (riders Ray Pickrell, Tony Jefferies, Mick Grant and Dave Croxford/ Alex George) 1975

Arguably the most famous TT machine ever built – indeed the only one to have its own nickname – and for a long time one of the most successful, Triumph's T150 Trident 'Slippery Sam' dominated the production class at the TT in the early 1970s. Yet even the five TT victories with which this remarkable machine is credited do not tell the whole story, for Sam is also believed to be the only motorcycle in the history of the TT to have won its class in five consecutive years. Amazingly, all of this was achieved against a backdrop of general British industrial decline, and a domestic motorcycle industry in a tailspin thanks to foreign imports. At the time, Solihull-based Triumph motorcycles (already incorporated into the BSA group) was struggling under the weight of competition from Japanese rivals, whose machines were more advanced and cheaper than British-made products. Nevertheless, on the race track the Triumph brand was still hugely successful, and in 1971 in the Production TT this factory-backed 750cc Trident, ridden by Ray Pickrell, stormed home to take the first of several victories.

The story of the Triumph Trident (and the machine built as a sister project, the BSA Rocket 3), is one of the most exasperating in the history of British motorcycles. The Trident might actually have been one of the few instances in which Triumph/ BSA could have been ahead of the curve with its planning. Yet because it took so many years to get from concept to prototype, then prototype to production, the window of opportunity had closed. Instead of being an incomparably fast, radically new machine, by the time it launched in late 1968 the Trident had already been eclipsed by the worldwide success of the Honda 750 Four.

In the late 1950s veteran engineers Herbert (Bert) Hopwood and Doug Hele had been struggling to produce more and more power from what were essentially the same designs that Triumph had been turning out since the end of the war. Bigger engines in the same frames produced vibration and handling problems, and heavier frames were not a solution in a racing context for obvious reasons. Then these talented designers came up with a radical new idea. Instead of trying to balance a powerful big twin with a 360-degree crank, what if they split the engine into three cylinders, and arrayed the crankshaft with pins every 120 degrees? In 1961, there were plenty of singles and twins, and even a few fours on the market. But no one else had a triple. The idea was wild, especially considering the conservative nature of BSA and Triumph management at the time. By 1962 they had drawn up all the engine internals and by 1965 they had a running prototype engine in a 650 Bonneville frame. If the machine had been released in 1966, before the Japanese had launched a successful big bike in the European and American markets, it might have secured Triumph's reputation as the pre-eminent performance machine manufacturer.

As it was, continued dithering by the management of parent company BSA caused the project to run on indefinitely, until the news of the forthcoming release of the Honda 750 Four forced their hand. One might think that after several years of tinkering with the prototype, the firm would have had something ready for market. In reality they were not even close. One reason was that the BSA hierarchy felt resentful of Triumph's greater popularity and success, and wanted to do something for their own dealers. So they insisted that the new Triumph Trident triple also be produced as a BSA, to be named the Rocket 3. However, instead of taking the easy route and producing a badge-engineered clone of the Trident, they took all the basic internals and put them into an entirely new set of engine cases. The only reason for this was to provide a fifteen-degree slant to the cylinders, in order to make the machine look different from the Triumph, which had vertical cylinders. However, that wasn't all. They also dropped it into an entirely new frame, completely different from that of the Trident unit. This ridiculous process (which was oddly typical of the British motor industry as a whole in the 1970s) slowed introduction and drove up costs.

However, BSA management didn't stop there. Bizarrely, they had come to the conclusion that this exciting new Triumph must not look anything like the highly successful Triumph twins of old. In order to achieve this, they subcontracted the styling of the bike to a firm that had never worked on a motorcycle before. The Ogle company had built their reputation in industrial design, and particularly in the motorcar business. One of their greatest claims was that they had styled the Reliant Robin, which was not a promising admission. This further delayed the release of the new bike, and predictably the final product was neither elegant nor beautiful. The new-for-1968 Triumph Trident and BSA Rocket 3 came to market with a clunky fuel tank so square that it quickly became known as the 'shoebox tank', along with slab-like side covers and silencers so outlandish they were nicknamed 'Flash Gordons' or 'Ray Guns'. Ironically, they worked very well, and were better than anything that came after. Many dedicated Triumph fans immediately began customising their machines, replacing the tank with something more elegant. Belatedly, on later models the company followed suit.

In the early 1970s the American market was still lucrative for British motorcycle manufacturers, and one of their biggest showcases was the Daytona 200 event. This was a race run under American Motorcycle Association rules, and suited anything production-based up to 750cc. Clearly it was a duplication of effort for Triumph, Norton et al to produce two sets of machines, one set up for the American races and another for the TT. In 1970 they succeeded in persuading the TT organisers to run a 750cc Production race, and it was in this arena that one particular Trident, nicknamed 'Slippery Sam', would make its mark. Leaving aside the fact that the Japanese were now making a major onslaught on all forms of motorsport, the financial situation at BSA and Triumph at that time meant that it was amazing that they accomplished anything at all, yet despite lacklustre sales in the showroom, on the racetrack the Triumph Trident was quickly proving to be a world-class winner.

Slippery Sam was one of three similar models built in the race shop at Triumph's Meriden works for the 1970 Production TT, one of which, ridden by Malcolm Uphill, won the race at 97.71mph. Tom Dickie was Sam's rider; he was a small man and the Triumph was big and, unused as he was to the foibles of the machine, he fumbled the Le Mans start and was last away. Nevertheless, he rode to finish a creditable fourth. The three Triumphs employed standard Trident frames, but within the limits of ACU regulations also utilised some of the Daytona modifications in their engines. There were Daytona-type valve gear-end camshafts, but the regulations did not permit the use of Daytona squish-type pistons. Sam earned his nickname around this time when, at a Bol d'Or race in France, the machine regurgitated oil all over its rider.

During the winter of 1970–71 the Triumph race shop had more time to devote to Sam's development. It now came under the special care of race shop mechanic Les Williams, who among other changes introduced a new frame, which though it looked standard was much lighter, having had all unnecessary lugs cut away. The Production class at the TT in those days was a different proposition from its equivalents today, and was more of a 'silhouette' category. A wide range of internal changes were allowed under the early 1970s rules and Slippery Sam featured higher compression, gas-flowed heads, racing cams and springs, close ratio gear clusters and better brakes. Beyond all this of course, there were also modifications that far exceeded what was allowed! The most significant of the rules that were bent were those forbidding a lighter frame, and that used by Sam meant that the machine overall tipped the scales at about 70lb under the standard Trident, which weighed in at around 470lb. Mick Grant remembered that Sam was:

> ...as legal as a bent copper – a real factory special full of bits that appeared in official Triumph parts lists but were unavailable to Joe Public at any price. It certainly felt a lot lighter and a lot faster than a standard Triumph triple.[41]

At the 1971 TT the legend of Sam began to grow as Ray Pickrell won the Production TT at a speed of 100.07mph, having clocked 142.3mph through a speed trap located on the drop down to the Highlander Inn. By 1972, the Triumph-BSA group was in serious financial difficulties and the decision was taken to drop all official support of production-based racing. Les Williams asked the firm if they would lend him Slippery Sam to enter privately at the TT, but an answer was slow in coming. Sadly Williams headed off to the TT that year as a mere spectator, but in a last-minute phonecall to Triumph management from his hotel, Williams persuaded them to release the machine. Amazingly, another Triumph factory mechanic named Fred Swift rode the motorcycle up to Liverpool to get it on a boat to the Island, and it actually started the race still with 'Tank Empty' stickers on from the crossing! Ray Pickrell won the race again, this time setting a new lap record of 101.61mph.

Les Williams was now maintaining the machine privately, though it remained officially Triumph property, but as it continued to win races he made an offer for it to his employers, which was accepted. Williams again arranged to be at the TT with Sam in 1973, and this time Tony Jefferies was so keen to ride the motorcycle that he actually offered to pay Williams's expenses. As always, the biggest threat came from Peter Williams and the Norton team. However, the old Norton weakness – the gearbox – meant that Williams dropped out while in the lead. After winning the race, Jefferies remarked, 'At Ramsey on the last lap I saw Peter sitting there and he looked so despondent that I gave the poor bloke a wave.'[42]

In 1974 the ACU tried to drop the production race from the TT schedule, but such were the protests from fans that it was reinstated. That year Mick Grant scored his first TT win aboard the Trident. The four-lap race was uneventful from a mechanical point of view, but not without drama in other areas. For a start, he rode with his right wrist in plaster after breaking a bone at a mainland meeting earlier in the season. Because of this, he was unable to grasp the throttle with his fingers. With his hand flat on the grip, he put the power on and off as if he was rolling pastry. Turning around during the race to check on the progress of the opposition, he lost all three perspex tear-offs from his visor, and had some difficulty seeing where he was going thereafter. Still, he roared to victory, remembering afterwards:

> Because of the pressure of time I only managed one lap in practice on the Triumph, and that's the only time I've ever raced a Production machine in the Isle of Man. I thought if I could keep Pete Williams in sight as far as Ramsey on the first lap I should be able to pass him on the Mountain climb. But as it worked out it was easier than I had hoped. I was in front before Ballacraine, and from then on it was a really enjoyable ride.[43]

He added later:

> That Trident never missed a beat throughout the TT race. It was a beautiful bike to ride and there's something magical about the sound of a Triumph three... Whenever I hear the wail of one being revved it always makes me think of the Isle of Man.[44]

In October 1974, the racer and journalist Ray Knight paid tribute not just to the power of the Triumph, but also its handling and other characteristics, stating in *Motorcyclist Illustrated* magazine:

> Isn't it amazing how the evergreen Trident 'Slippery Sam' keeps on winning the big production races? For the last four years that bike has had enough performance to blow everything else into the weeds. Not just mph but sheer 'bikeability', now part of current jargon and defined as the optimum combination of handling, braking and torque characteristics that makes it a winner.[45]

Strangely, Triumph made little attempt to cash in on the success of Slippery Sam and there was never a road-legal replica or over-the-counter version. Any such plans that the firm might have had would almost certainly have turned to ashes with the final collapse of BSA/Triumph in 1973, and the absorption of the remnants into the semi-nationalised Norton-Villiers-Triumph (NVT) group. However, it is to the 1975 Production race that we now turn our attention. For this event the race had been extended to ten laps, with two riders sharing the workload. Alex George and Dave Croxford took Sam to its fifth and final victory, in the process breaking the lap record already held by

Mick Grant aboard Slippery Sam in 1974. Mick thought the bike about 'as legal as a bent copper'! (Bikesport Fottofinders archives)

the machine and extending it to an extraordinary 102.82mph. Alex George remembered afterwards:

It was a fantastic feeling when I caught and passed Chas Mortimer and we were in the lead. I'd been talking to him in the pits before we both went out to do the final three laps. At that time I didn't think we had a cat in hell's chance of winning but we knew it would be close – and as Chas went out he said, 'OK, it's between the two of us – let's have a go'. It's a real pleasure to race against a man like Chas. I've a great respect for him. I was getting signals from three places on each lap so I realised after I'd done one of those three laps that I could catch him if I pressed on. That was when I did the record lap. I'd really got the feel of the bike and it was the first time I'd drifted a Triumph. I've never been around Greeba Castle so fast. What a motorcycle.

On the last lap I wasn't expecting to catch Chas until the Mountain. But I glimpsed a bike after Glen Helen and I finally caught him just above Sarah's Cottage. I waved my foot at him – and immediately cut my revs from 8,000 to 7,000 – the race was in the bag. The people round the course were going wild – standing on the banks and waving. I knew it was Slippery Sam they wanted to win and it was a great boost.[46]

It was one of the final flourishes of the old British motorcycle industry. By 1976, Slippery Sam was ineligible to continue competing in the Production class at the TT, due to the fact that the machine was now more than five years old. Sam ended its days at the National Motorcycle Museum in Birmingham, where after some years on display it was destroyed in the disastrous 2003 fire, which gutted part of the museum.

A replica, made by technicians at the now resurgent Triumph company, stands in its place. As one of the most recognisable and successful machines of any era at the TT (not just the 1970s), Slippery Sam has become almost a part of the folklore of the event, and while there are still people around like Grant and George who rode the machine and always speak fondly of it, it will never truly be gone.

Triumph Trident Slippery Sam, before it was destroyed in the disastrous National Motorcycle Museum fire. (Author's collection)

Chapter 13

750cc Windle Yamaha sidecar outfit (riders George O'Dell/Kenny Arthur) 1977

In the 1960s, the sidecar events at the TT had largely been dominated by German and Swiss riders on BMW-engined outfits. However, by the mid-1970s British drivers had begun a fightback, which was to a large extent due to the arrival of the Yamaha TZ750 engine. It was affordable, easily obtainable, reliable and worked well in a sidecar outfit. The man who would take this engine, together with a Windle chassis, into the TT history books was George O'Dell, when in 1977, together with passenger Kenny Arthur, he broke the 100mph barrier for sidecars in the Isle of Man, in the same year that he secured the sidecar world championship. It was one of the most memorable events in sidecar history and O'Dell, though his TT career was short, was one of the most colourful characters that the sport has produced. This chapter examines the story of his 1977 record-breaking outfit.

George O'Dell was born in Hemel Hempstead in 1945, and worked as an engineer at Kents Brushworks. He had been a leather-clad rocker in his youth, until an accident on his road bike lessened his interest in two-wheelers, and instead he began to consider three. O'Dell's involvement in sidecar racing quickly grew. He made his Isle of Man debut in 1970, but the 1971 TT was almost his last, as a bad crash put both O'Dell and his passenger in hospital. Many of his early rides were on BSA machinery, before converting to König two-stroke technology like a number of his contemporaries. O'Dell's fiery character made him determined to make his mark on the Grand Prix scene, and in 1975 his attitude made an impression on Eric May, a Berkshire businessman who became a major sponsor. It was May who purchased for O'Dell his first TZ engine, acquired through a Swiss Yamaha importer.

Having the Yamaha engine alone, however, was not enough to bring success. O'Dell used it with a chassis made by one of the greatest constructors in British sidecar history, Terry Windle. A machinist by trade, Windle started racing solos in 1961, with his first race being at Rhydymwyn in Wales. His solo career was short-lived as he soon took up sidecar racing. This led to him building his own chassis in his garage before opening up his own workshop in the village of Thurgoland. His sidecar chassis-building career spanned over forty years, and even after officially retiring in 2008 he continued to build bikes in the garage behind his house. His chassis won five world championships with riders George O'Dell, Jock Taylor, Darren Dixon and Steve Abbott (twice). O'Dell began using the Windle outfit almost by accident. He had sold his previous machine in 1975 and had intended to build his own hub-centred steering outfit. However, he did not complete it in time for the 1976 season, and purchased the Windle as a stop-gap. It proved a good move – as O'Dell later commented, Windle machinery was ideally suited for the bumpy TT circuit. However, 1976 was not a great year. His regular passenger was badly injured in a collision with a wall, and he returned home from the TT with nothing. At the same time, however, he was making progress and gaining experience in Grands Prix events in Europe, and acquired a new passenger in the form of Kenny Arthur, a maintenance engineer with Lever Brothers on Merseyside. For the 1977 season O'Dell put all he had into the purchase of a Seymaz chassis, which would be his main outfit. The trusty Windle remained his back up, and with the Seymaz damaged at Cadwell Park in the spring of 1977, it took centre stage at that year's TT. Unlike the previous year, when it had appeared in the yellow and green livery of main sponsor BP, this time it was in the distinctive yellow and red of Shell. So highly was O'Dell regarded, that the rival oil company had made him a financial offer he simply could not refuse. Passenger Kenny Arthur remembered:

The Windle was a very stable bike particularly around the Isle of Man. It was well-proven... Lots of people had used them and you felt very confident on the bike. It was one of those bikes you could change direction on it and not feel endangered in any way – and nicely put together, it was really well engineered. Compared to the bikes today I don't suppose it was, but it just felt right. It felt very right. The circuit was a lot bumpier then, and some of the corners were a lot tighter, but the bike was good... It was a four-cylinder two-stroke Yamaha, 750cc, which was the same engine that we used for Grands Prix, only you put 250 cylinders and pistons and exhausts on it, which took it down to a 500 for Grands Prix. Grands Prix were always 500cc at that particular time, and internationals were 750 or 700 depending on what cylinders you used. But it was a lovely bike, very kind, very reliable. And George did the engine, I never touched the engine at all. We had one mechanic who came with us to do the chassis, which I was quite capable of doing, but they did it down south and so they were more familiar with it than I was, and I wasn't so much hands on at that particular time with the mechanic-ing for George because the bike was pretty much ready, I think it was everything else that wasn't ready, the bike was always done first![47]

George O'Dell in thoughtful mood at the 1977 TT, seated aboard the Windle Yamaha outfit on which he broke the 100mph barrier. (Courtesy of Ken Sprayson)

O'Dell went to the 1977 TT in the middle of his campaign for the world championship title. Although this was the first time that a TT win would carry no title points, the two sidecar races on the Isle of Man were still eagerly anticipated and certain to be hotly contested. The first practice session on the

Island demonstrated just how severely an outfit could be battered by the bumpy roads – the Windle came back to the pits with a main chassis tube broken, a loose rear sprocket and a crack to a rear suspension mount. It took an all-night session in a rented garage in Douglas to put the damage right, but the outfit was ready for the second sidecar practice the following afternoon. O'Dell and the mechanics also made a series of modifications, including going up a jet size on the carburettor to 310 instead of the 300 used on the UK circuits, in order to give more power on the climb up the mountain. They had also used a harder spark plug, an N82G, in order to prevent it melting with the heat and possibly dropping into the cylinder, and opted to put a size 19 sprocket (the largest) on the engine with the smallest possible (a 33) on the rear wheel. When it was airborne, the engine would rev to an additional 1000rpm before the back wheel bit into the road again, pulling the engine back with enormous force as it did so. All of that force was transferred through the chain, and at the Isle of Man TT a chain could stretch by as much as the length of a link over several laps. To help cope with this, chain manufacturer Renold had supplied O'Dell with an experimental version made of harder steel, which reduced stretching considerably. There was nothing experimental or revolutionary about his tyres, however: they were standard Goodyear G50 slicks. The radiator was from a cannibalised Suzuki road bike, fitted because it was considerably lighter than the Yamaha equivalent, and at a slight angle in order to minimise the damage caused by stones flicked out from the rear wheel of an outfit in front.

The magical 100mph sidecar lap had almost been achieved in 1976, when Mac Hobson and Mick Burns had lapped at 99.962mph. Now there was much speculation as to whether 1977 would see the barrier broken. With the bike back in good order and with his familiarity with the Mountain Circuit returning after a year away, O'Dell felt confident enough to push things as hard as he could during the second practice. After the first two laps O'Dell pulled into the pits to check that everything was still in place on the bike, and to make sure that his passenger Kenny Arthur was comfortable with the performance so far. On the third lap, from a standing start O'Dell launched the pairing into the history books, achieving an incredible 101.30mph. O'Dell remembered:

> It wasn't hard. There wasn't too much traffic out at the time, and any sidecars I did meet I seemed to catch at the best places to overtake without any trouble. There were a few corners that I went through very quickly, at a speed I didn't think a sidecar could go through. Quarry Bends we sailed through just like greased lightning. At Cronk Y Voddy and Sulby, I went through fairly gently because those straights are so bumpy. I got a bit of elevation at Ballaugh Bridge which I normally do through failing to

brake early enough. Over the Mountain I seemed to flash past the 32nd and 33rd milestones. Always have liked the Mountain section. But there were no problems at all. Didn't even get near any kerbs or grass.[48]

Everything went so smoothly. I thought it was a good lap on the descent from the Mountain, coming down from Kate's Cottage to the Creg. The rest of the way home I knew there was only one place where there might be a hold up – Governor's Bridge. But there was only one bloke to pass after Governor's. Had we caught him going into Governor's he might have cost us 20 seconds, which would have killed the lap. I'd watched Kenny out of the corner of my eye, flashing around, and I could tell he was enjoying himself. As I braked hard for Governor's the smell of burning brakes told me it must be a fast lap. I took it through the gears to 10,500rpm as I screwed it over the line. You can waste five seconds by rolling it off at the finish. I overshot the gate to the paddock and we had to wheel it backwards.[49]

For Kenny Arthur as well there was an instinctive feeling that this lap was 'the one'. He remembered:

It didn't feel a lot different or a lot harder, [but] it was obvious that the bike was very quick in a straight line, and at the Isle of Man that's quite critical, because you knew by the bumps and the bangs that you were getting going round various places [it] was a lot quicker than you had ever been before, so it was pretty obvious that we were very close; there and thereabouts for doing the 100 mile an hour. I'd been very close once before so I had a good idea what it was going to be like, and it was good, it was OK... I felt very confident, I never felt in trouble with George at any state in my racing career ever, he would always seem to be in control, so I didn't have any qualms or questions, I just got on with the job... When we got back we were quite shocked really. As soon as we rolled up in the paddock the boss of the Beresford [Hotel], John, he had a bottle of champagne, they were all standing there cheering and shouting, they said 'you've done it, you've done it'. So, OK it was in practice, but it was done, and when we got back to the hotel they'd painted all the windows... It felt really good, really special. You don't realise until later in your life how special that moment was, it's all in an adrenaline rush and 'of the moment'. After the moment you realise what a part of TT history that was.[50]

A record lap in practice is always considered to be 'unofficial', but for O'Dell that day it made no difference. When the timing officials showed him the pink slip with his time noted on it he knew that he had achieved a personal ambition that he had been chasing since his crash at the TT in 1971. Since then, O'Dell's respect for the circuit had only increased, but at the same time so had his determination to conquer it. When he learned of his achievement there were tears in his eyes, and that night he returned to the race office to stare at the practice leaderboard notice in the window, unable to take his eyes off his time, before returning to the team lodgings at the Beresford Hotel where a party in his honour was in full swing.

For the first sidecar race of that 1977 TT O'Dell had been allocated the number sixteen, which greatly annoyed him. By rights he should have been in the top handful, but with a number as high as that he would have perhaps six crews to pass on the road before having a clear track in front of him, severely limiting his prospects in the race. His protests to the ACU fell on deaf ears, and there was nothing for it but for driver and passenger to equip themselves with a number of tear-off visors; there was a distinct possibility that they might get stuck behind another outfit blowing out oil mist and be unable to pass them for several miles. His chief opposition came in the form of Dick Greasley, with passenger Mick Skeels, and West German driver Rolf Steinhausen with passenger Wolfgang Kalauch. It was a four-lap race with a pit stop, and in the first two laps O'Dell encountered heavy traffic on the road, which caused him to lose concentration and affected his speed. When he pitted, things got worse, with first a jammed fuel filler nozzle and then fuel accidentally spilled all over the passenger platform, which had to be cleaned up if Kenny Arthur was to have any chance of staying onboard. The fuel was two-stroke mixture and Kenny remembered:

> It got a bit slippy, because there was oil in it and unfortunately we couldn't wipe it up. It was what they called a 'splash and dash' – it was a gallon in and then push off and you're ready to go. The other thing is, with a hot two-stroke engine, they really take a lot of pushing, and when you've just done two laps it's hard going. We pushed and pushed and then it fired up and we were gone, so it was good. It was a little bit slippy under foot, but I just managed to keep hold of the handles, I think that was important because it got on my leathers and on my knees, and with it having oil in the petrol I was sliding about a bit.[51]

Even being told that Greasley had already lapped at over 100mph did not phase O'Dell; if anything it made him more determined, and on the next lap he settled into the job in hand. On the third lap he overhauled Steinhausen, and at Ballaugh a board told him he had a lead of two seconds over Greasley. By the final lap that was up to forty seconds and eventually, although he never managed to pass him or even catch him on the road, O'Dell took the race from Greasley by fifty seconds. In the process he had pushed up the sidecar lap record to 102.80mph. He remembered:

> The crowd made me do 102.80mph. As I was catching different guys, people could see me coming and would wave like mad at these other drivers, telling them to move over. It was incredible. During the last lap I was lapping the late starters and, at Ramsey, the crowd went wild as they urged two slower outfits to let me through. Talk about being switched on. The Island was being great to me and everything was going as smooth as silk. On the last lap... I experienced one of my best feelings in racing. The spectators were urging me on, everyone seemed to be waving. At the Gooseneck where you're going slowly, you're almost in personal contact with the crowd who are just a few feet away. I could tell they were with me. They wanted me to catch Dick on the road – they knew he wasn't far ahead of me. Going through Brandish and Hillberry I thought some of them were going to get on my bike. They were going crazy and at Governor's I could hear them shouting.[52]

Everyone in the pits was elated. John Thompson from the Beresford Hotel had a Rolls-Royce waiting with champagne and took the team back to the hotel, where more supporters were eager to greet the two and congratulate them on their achievement. The Windle outfit was battered on its return to the pits – the engine was worn out and had to be replaced before the next race, and a number of cracks to the chassis had to be welded. Kenny Arthur had taken a buffeting and had to visit an osteopath for treatment before the second race.

Race 2 was set to be another trailblazer and O'Dell was leading on time when the smell of burning clutch alerted him to possible problems. At Ballaugh the engine gave up the ghost, and he and Arthur spent the rest of the race in the Raven pub. O'Dell's main concern was that someone else would take his lap record, but he need not have worried. Even greater glory was to come for the Windle Yamaha later that year in the British Sidecar Grand Prix at Silverstone. O'Dell's other machine, a Seymaz, proved unreliable and so it was aboard his TT-winning outfit that he clinched the necessary points to secure the 1977 Sidecar World Championship, the first British competitor to do so for twenty-four years. Amazingly, O'Dell's championship came without him ever having won a race, so consistent was he in securing podium positions, and it was a strange irony that the only race he did win that year – the Isle of Man TT – no longer counted towards a world title.

Sadly, in 1981 George O'Dell lost his life in a house fire after a stand-off with the police. Some blame the break up of his marriage, others his difficulties in

George O'Dell and Kenny Arthur after victory in one of the greatest-ever sidecar TT races, the 1977 500cc race. (Courtesy of Christine Arthur)

finding sponsorship. Whatever lay behind his death, sidecar racing lost one of its greatest exponents that day. It is not clear what became of his Windle outfit, but no part of it now appears to exist. In 2005 Manx sidecar constructor Dave Molyneux spent many months looking for it, and despite following up several promising leads was eventually forced to conclude that it did not survive. What is fairly certain is that at the end of 1977 O'Dell took it to the United States to take part in an exhibition race and turned it over in a 90mph accident that left him with serious injuries. A steel pin was inserted into his badly broken leg, and it was only after four weeks of recuperation that O'Dell was able to fly home. The machine, though badly damaged, was air-freighted back to the UK, and was then sold by O'Dell. It was later reported that a subsequent owner also crashed it, and this time wrote it off. It was a sad end for one of the greatest three-wheelers ever – a machine that broke the 100mph barrier and won a world championship in the same year, and that makes it into the top twenty-five TT machines with ease. The closest we may ever come to seeing it roar into life might be to watch the almost exact replica built by Dave Molyneux for the 2007 TT Parade Lap, which was described by the late Terry Windle as 'uncannily similar' to the original machine. That replica is now in the hands of a Suffolk collector.

Chapter 14

Sports Motorcycles 900cc Ducati (rider Mike Hailwood) 1978

1978 was truly a vintage year at the TT, as the event produced two of our top twenty-five greatest TT machines. Number fourteen in our rundown is also the second of three in this book to be associated with the great Mike Hailwood. This machine is the one with which he made his legendary 1978 comeback to the TT, the 900cc Ducati aboard which he won the Formula 1 race that year. The machine was supplied by Steve Wynne, of Manchester independent dealers Sports Motorcycles. Wynne himself had raced Italian-made Ducatis with some success in the mid-1970s, but in his own judgment, as the pressure of building up the business drew more heavily on his time, he was better off working on the bikes rather than riding them. Yet for Wynne, achieving a victory at the Isle of Man TT remained an unfulfilled ambition.

The first time he tried his hand as a team manager was at the 1976 event, when with riders Roger Nicholls and Steve Tonkin his Ducati 750SS built an imposing lead in the ten-lap Production TT, only for a piston to fail with one lap to go. With the loss of world championship status the following year, 1977 saw the inauguration of the TT Formula 1 class, allowing competitors a greater degree of engine-tuning than under the old Production rules, as well as, significantly, complete freedom of chassis design. The cynics claimed that the class was introduced in order to keep the Japanese factories interested, by allowing them to be competitive on a road course, where their powerful but poorly handling street bikes had yet to prove themselves. To relate the two categories to modern classes, Production racing was essentially the same as Superstock, whereas TT Formula 1 was Superbike racing without the need to use stock frames and silhouette bodywork – only a highly modified production street engine.

For 1977 Wynne had persuaded the Ducati factory to sell him an ex-works 900SS-based endurance racer to use in the TT Formula 1 race. The bike arrived at the last minute, leaving the Sports Motorcycles team little time to prepare it, but nevertheless Roger Nicholls threatened to beat the works Honda of former world champion Phil Read before the distance was abruptly cut short, handing the race to the Japanese firm and along with it a world title. Yet revenge would not be long in coming, albeit from a completely unexpected source.

In far away New Zealand, Mike Hailwood, in enforced retirement following a serious crash in Formula 1 car racing at the Nürburgring, was contemplating a return to racing motorcycles. His crippled foot meant that he could no longer heel-and-toe the pedals of a car, but that would not be a problem on a motorbike. Mike didn't need the money (even though he was subsequently offered substantial amounts). His father (a double millionaire) had recently died, and Mike was financially secure. But he was restless, and he needed a challenge. Mike began to test his competitiveness by entering some minor races in Australia. Gradually, he made up his mind to try his hand at the TT again. Ted Macauley, *Daily Mirror* journalist and a friend of Hailwood, remembers that when he first wrote to him to tell him of his plans to return to the TT, Macauley thought he was mad. When he met up with him again at Manchester airport, not having seen him in a couple of years, his worst fears were confirmed. Hailwood looked like he had gone to seed; he had lost most of his hair, he walked with a limp and enforced idleness had given him a pot belly. Nevertheless, he convinced Macauley that he could get back to reasonable fitness. As for Macauley's concerns about the dangers of what he was proposing, Mike assured him that it would be nothing too serious, and that his main objective was simply to have a little fun back at his old stamping ground; he then asked him if he would arrange things with the ACU. Naturally, with the TT struggling following the loss of world championship status in 1976, both the Isle of Man government, and ACU supremo Vernon Cooper, were delighted to have this endorsement from Britain's most revered racer, and agreed to the proposed starting fee.

It is a common misconception that Mike's initial outing in practice at the 1978 TT was his first lap of the Island since 1967. In fact, Mike had not been idle and, at the 1977 MGP, under the guise of filming a documentary, he had completed a few laps on closed roads. Having decided that he could be competitive, in typical Hailwood fashion he aimed to put his all into it. What happened next was one of those happy coincidences that fate sometimes delivers. Steve Wynne takes up the story:

A couple of months after the '77 TT, we went to Silverstone for Roger Nicholls to ride in the TT F1 support race at the British GP. In the paddock there I was introduced to Mike Hailwood, who was visiting

Britain from New Zealand, where he'd been living since retiring from Formula 1 car racing after his 1974 smash at the Nürburgring. He sees the Ducati, slings his leg over it, and says 'This is the kind of old fashioned bike I understand – wouldn't mind doing another TT on this!' Half-jokingly, I say 'Why don't you?!' – and with just a few words and a hand shake, the deal is done, for a paltry, completely nominal rider's fee of £1000 – I used to think it was even less, but I just discovered our single-sheet contract, complete with Mike's witticisms scrawled on it, in a drawer! But essentially Mike just wanted to have an enjoyable ride back in the Island he loved racing in – his plan was originally to ride under an assumed name, thinking nobody would realise it was him. Some hope![53]

Remembering what had happened last time, Wynne immediately contacted Ducati, even though there were still ten months to go before the 1978 TT, in order to get a machine in good time to work on it. In fact, this time he ordered two brand-new motorcycles. Wynne agreed to pay separately for the bikes, one up front and the other at the end of that year, and they arrived (painted in the firm's standard colours of red and silver) in good time, before the end of 1977. There was one each for Hailwood and regular rider Roger Nicholls, who after his efforts in the previous two years was actually thought of as Sports Motorcycles' best hope for victory, since Hailwood had not raced a bike at a top level event since his appearance at Daytona aboard a BSA Rocket in the early 1970s. Indeed for Mike the Sports Motorcycles deal was something of a sideshow, for his main effort at the 1978 TT was to be made as part of the Martini racing team, with Yamaha sponsorship. Yamaha were to supply him with three machines, as against Sports Motorcycles' one.

Having the bikes early meant that Wynne could prepare them carefully. His changes involved reworking the heads with larger valves, changing pistons, ignition, clutch and most importantly the gear cluster, which was the major weakness of a racing Ducati in the mid-1970s. That this was possible was entirely due to the esteem in which Hailwood was held in car racing circles as well as motorcycle ones. The new gears were made by a contact of Mike's from his Formula 1 car racing days, Mike Hewland at Hewland Gears, who made all the gearboxes for the British F1 teams. However, whereas this service would normally have commanded a five-figure fee, Hewland redesigned and manufactured the new gear ratios purely as a favour. Later the information was passed on to Ducati, for free, and they incorporated much of the design into their future road models.

Other changes that Wynne made included reworking the crankshaft. His experience with Ducatis told him that the big-end would tend to fail when the engine was driven hard. To compensate for this an oversized crankpin was made up and pressed into the standard flywheel. The standard rods were retained, but machined out to accept new big end rollers. Finally the rods were polished and smoothed. Because pistons could also break up under heavy use he replaced these with some specially imported from America. These were Teflon coated and with a raised crown, to bring the compression ratio up to 11:1. In order to accept these slightly larger pistons the barrels also had to be slightly rebored. The heavier pistons also meant that the crankshaft had to be rebalanced, and rather than add weight to achieve this he chose to shave metal away from around the crankpin. He also worked on the camshaft. The timing of the standard factory race engine was not particularly precise, so he machined two extra keyways into the timing bevel gears and this, combined with offset keys, allowed the cams to be set up spot on. The two Sports Motorcycles bikes were also re-liveried in red, white and green paint, a colour scheme that Wynne based on a can of Castrol oil. Castrol were one of Mike's other sponsors, and the decision had nothing at all to do with the colours of the Italian flag, even though Ducati later claimed that they did!

Though it was a dream come true to be working with Mike Hailwood, the pressure on Wynne was immense. He had hundreds of letters before the race from Hailwood fans, some threatening to hold him personally responsible if Mike were to be killed or injured. As an illustration of the level of interest and anticipation that existed at the time, *Motor Cycle News* accidentally published a reversed print of the Ducati without the bodywork on, which gave the false impression that the sump plug was wired up the wrong way. This caused some forty or fifty people to write to or phone the Manchester dealer, telling them of the apparent error. Further evidence of the 'Hailwood effect' was noticeable on the Isle of Man, where every hotel room during the TT was booked up months in advance once his return was confirmed, and it was said that in 1978 his name brought an additional 50,000 visitors to the Island.

During pre-race testing and TT practice the engine tuned by Sports Motorcycles proved to be fast and reliable – Hailwood topped the leaderboard during Formula 1 practice with a new lap record at 111mph, but was convinced that he had only done 105mph or thereabouts, because the Ducati felt so relaxed and easy to ride. During practice, two Ducati factory race engineers, Franco Farne and Giuliano Pedretti, had arrived on the Island from Bologna to watch and help out if necessary. Farne became concerned about the high mileage that the engine had put in during practice, and persuaded Wynne to fit a new one that they had brought over with them. Mike did a solitary lap with this engine on Friday night, the day before the race.

Leaving their hotel the following morning, Hailwood and Macauley drove up to the grandstand together, the former already in his leathers, both deep in thought. Eventually, Macauley broke the silence by telling Hailwood that he thought he had been lying to him. Puzzled, the rider asked in what way, and his mentor replied that he thought Hailwood had not just come back to the TT for some fun, but that in fact he really was set on trying to win. 'Too bloody right I'm going to try to win!' he replied. Macauley had arranged for Hailwood to go out as number twelve, partly as a nod to the fact that he had won twelve TT races up to that point. There was also clever thinking behind the plan, in that Hailwood would not be going out too near the front. If he could work his way up through the field all well and good, but if he finished further back they could always blame the bike and this would avoid potential embarrassment. Starting as number one in the Formula 1 TT that morning was his old sparring partner from the 1960s, Phil Read, riding for Honda Britain. As the race progressed, Hailwood worked his way through the pack and caught Read on the approach to Ramsey. Having diced with him a little, Mike, ever the showman, took the opportunity to pass Read in Parliament Square in front of hundreds of cheering fans, delighted to see their hero take the lead. Seconds beforehand, however, catastrophe had only just been averted when, as the two entered Ramsey, a large black Labrador dog appeared in the middle of the road on the approach to Parliament Square. A marshal chased it towards Bircham Avenue, having to pin himself against the wall as the two came past: he had literally nowhere to go to get out of the way, the timing was that close. The two riders were side by side, and if either of them had hit the dog it would have been a disaster. As the race progressed, Hailwood finally forced Read's machine to over-rev, and he dropped out.

In the event, although it was good enough to win the race, the Bologna factory engine proved to be much slower than the Sports Motorcycles motor, and blew up when the bottom bevel gear on the rear cylinder disintegrated just as Mike shut off to cross the finish line and win. Because of pressure from the FIM there was a strict noise control at the TT that year, and all the finishers were supposed to be tested at the end of the race. There had been some doubt about whether the Ducati would pass, even with the Triumph silencers that had been spliced on to the Lafranconi exhausts. However, the noise meter man didn't want to be strung up for being the one to disqualify Hailwood after his famous TT comeback win, so as the bike was pushed back to the parc fermé there came a rhetorical question, 'The engine won't start, will it?!'. Wynne was happy to agree. Ironically, he would not discover that this was actually true until much

Mike Hailwood aboard the Sports Motorcycles Ducati with which he took his thirteenth TT win in spectacular fashion – the 1978 Formula 1 race. (Bikesport Fottofinders archives)

later, when he learned of the damage to the cylinder! Wynne has one other personal memory of that memorable victory:

> I've never considered myself to be superstitious, but this was one occasion that makes me wonder. The atmosphere throughout practice was electric, because Honda were going all out to retain their title, and besides Phil Read had the likes of Tom Herron, Tony Rutter, John Williams and Helmut Dähne on works bikes or dealer entries, with only our Ducatis and Chas Mortimer on a Suzuki to stop them. But there was some good-natured banter between Read and Hailwood, and just before the start of the race, Phil came over to wish Mike and myself good luck, and in typical cheeky form suggested I ought to support him by wearing a Phil Read T-shirt! I did in fact take off my Sports Motorcycles/Hailwood T-shirt and spent

the whole of the race in the pits apparently supporting our greatest rival, till at the end of the last lap, Mike's light came on at Signpost Corner miles in the lead, to tell us we were almost home and dry. Only then, realising I still had the Phil Read T-shirt on, did I start to take it off to don our own team colours, ready to welcome Mike as the victor. But Giuliano Pedretti, the Ducati works mechanic, stopped me as I did so: 'Keep it on,' he said, 'or it may cause bad luck'. I wonder to this day, if I'd removed the T-shirt, would the timing gear have broken at Governor's Bridge just a few hundred yards from the finish, instead of just on the line?![54]

Hailwood recounted afterwards his own emotions, as the 'Boy's Own' adventure of returning to the TT and winning once again began to become reality:

It was terrible in a way, everybody was waving to me, just as they had been from the very start. I'd never known that before – but when I started on the last lap I had my heart in my mouth all the way round. People were waving and jumping up and down, but I didn't return a single wave. I kept my hands on the grips, kept my concentration turned on and hoped against all hope that nothing would go wrong. It was by far the longest lap I've ever known at the TT. I couldn't wait for it to end. I could not bring myself to speed it up, or slow it down. I just kept on going at what I hoped was a normal sort of lick. As I got closer to the chequered flag the tears started to stream down my face. I was so full up with the emotion of it all, with the reaction I could see from the crowds lining the road and the cheers I could hear even over the noise of the engine, that I couldn't help myself. When I saw the finish line looming up I could not believe I had done it, in fact it didn't really hit me until about three weeks later.[55]

On his way to the winner's enclosure with his very relieved friend and manager, Ted Macauley, Hailwood was overwhelmed by the enormity of it all, and, fighting back the tears, gasped: 'I've had some wins, here and in the rest of the world, but for sheer emotion this beats them all. I can't explain how I feel. It's beyond all my dreams. Unbelievable.'[56]

As he climbed the steps to the podium, took his hat off and turned to wave to the crowd, he had evidently lost the battle with his emotions, and was clearly seen to wipe a tear from his eye. He received the congratulations of second-place man John Williams, as well as the adulation of the crowd, who could not believe what they had just seen. After a celebratory drink back at the hotel, Hailwood took a quick bath to ease away the aches of the day, before heading off to a restaurant where a party in his honour was in full swing. At the end of the week, Mike was voted 'Man of the Meeting' by a panel of journalists, though modest as ever, he gave the trophy to Mick Grant.

The Ducati, however, was not finished yet. The following weekend Mike went to the post-TT meeting at Mallory Park for the TT Formula 1 British title round. The team refitted the original Sports Motorcycles engine that Mike had practised with in the Island to use in the race, in which he beat future British champion John Cowie on the P&M Kawasaki, as well as Phil Read and all his TT rivals once again. In some ways this was an even greater feat than the TT win, because the Japanese bikes were nimbler and had better acceleration than the long-wheelbase Ducati, which made them better suited to such a short, tight-cornering circuit. Yet again Hailwood's brilliance made the difference. They did two more British TT Formula 1 races together that year, at Donington where Mike crashed while in the lead and wrote off the fairing – afterwards the crowd swarmed over the machine like ants, trying to to pick up pieces of the broken bodywork to keep as souvenirs! – and the other at Silverstone in the British Grand Prix support race, where on this fastest of British mainland circuits Cowie got his revenge and Mike was simply out-powered. He finished third.

The maestro himself later downplayed his TT victory, writing in *Racing and all That* in 1980 that really it should not have been possible for him to win again after so long out of the game, but he had two major advantages. Firstly he knew every inch of the circuit – the location of every bump and dip – whereas he felt that the late 1970s generation of riders had not done enough to learn the course, as he had in the 1960s. The second advantage was that he felt that many were not trying as hard as they might, for financial reasons. Quite a number of them were worried about the cost implications if they blew up an engine.

At the end of 1978 Steve Wynne sold the Hailwood Ducati, unrestored and as used – complete with Donington crash scrapes – to a Japanese collector, and from then on the tale of this machine becomes one of intrigue. This was the same engine and chassis – both bearing the number 088238 – that Mike had used at Mallory, Donington and Silverstone, and therefore the same chassis he won the TT with too, and most people agree that it is the chassis that determines the identity of a motorbike. Mike Hailwood sat in that seat to win the TT, and nobody else ever did so on a race track after that Silverstone meeting. The second Sports Motorcycles 1978 bike, the one that Roger Nicholls rode in the TT when he retired with a broken oil level inspection window, was purchased from the factory by the main British Ducati importers at that time, who then refused to sell it on to Steve Wynne under the terms of his original deal with Ducati. Instead, they turned it into the first 'Hailwood TT-winner' forgery. They later sold it to a German enthusiast with a letter certifying it was the Hailwood bike, which it clearly never was. Mike had not ridden even a single practice lap on the bike, and in any case the importers had no involvement whatsoever with Hailwood's race effort, so they could not possibly have known which bike was which.

Meanwhile, Ducati decided to launch the Mike Hailwood Replica 900SS roadbike the following year. Neither Mike nor Wynne were paid any royalties for it, even though over 7,000 were built and sold over a seven-year period. Ironically, this model was so commercially successful that it saved the state-owned factory from near-certain bankruptcy (and did so in Castrol colours!). A year or so later, the next con-artist appeared on the scene and contacted Steve Wynne from the USA, claiming to be the world's biggest Hailwood fan. He begged for even a nut or bolt from the original Hailwood bike, which might still have been lying around, to place in his Hailwood shrine. Taking him at face value, Wynne revealed that he still had the TT-winning engine, even though it had been heavily modified in the meantime, plus a spare wheel and a damaged fork slider that had been salvaged from the Donington crash. He sold the items for just a few pounds, thinking little more of it. A year or so later 'The Original TT-Winning Mike Hailwood Ducati' was put up for sale in the USA, completely cloned from just a cracked crankcase and a broken fork slider! After correspondence between Wynne and the buyer of this fake, the purchaser sued the man who created it and the bike ended up in the hands of a third party, who broke it up and offered the cracked crankcases and other modified parts for sale once more.

Meanwhile, in 1996 the genuine bike reappeared from Japan and was sold at auction in Los Angeles to Larry and Mark Aurtiana. Steve Wynne was sure that this was the genuine machine he had sold to Japan for a paltry £5,000 in 1978, and he tried unsuccessfully to buy it back at the auction in 1996, with a losing bid of £80,000. This in fact guarantees its authenticity, for Wynne would be unlikely to put up that much money to buy a forgery! The original engine with matching numbers that came with the bike when new is still installed in it – the one which Mike used in practice at the TT and won the race with at Mallory – together with every nut, bolt and washer that he raced with during the 1978 season. Odd bits do exist elsewhere, which were used at some stage by Mike, but that's the nature of wear and tear in racing. This motorcycle is history on wheels, and now resides in the Ducati museum in Bologna, proudly exhibited by the manufacturers in a display that celebrates their finest racing moment.

The Hailwood Ducati today, in the company's Bologna museum. (Author's collection)

The Hailwood Ducati makes it into the top twenty-five TT machines with ease. Few other motorcycles have such a compelling backstory, beginning with the engineering skill required to turn what was originally a fairly standard factory racing machine into something exceptional, which was capable of outpacing the fastest motorcycle that a giant like Honda could pit against it. Then there is the amazing story of Hailwood himself and his return to the scene of his earlier triumphs. Even some of his greatest fans initially doubted that he could rediscover the form he had displayed in his youth. Finally there is the intrigue that has surrounded the bike and its identity. It is a testament to the significance of this machine that so many people were prepared to try to clone it or claim it as their own, and that the road-going replica that Ducati produced was such a phenomenal success that examples are now collectors' pieces in their own right.

Chapter 15

750cc Kawasaki (rider Mick Grant) 1978

Despite his early association with the famous Triumph 'Slippery Sam', and his later success as a Suzuki works rider, Yorkshireman Mick Grant's name will be forever linked with the so-called 'Green Meanie' Kawasakis that he rode at the TT in the mid-1970s. Grant was born near Wakefield, the son of a coal miner. From an early age he knew that he did not want to follow in his father's footsteps, and as a lad he began messing about with motorcycles. Pretty soon he was hooked, and while at art college he began developing his skills as a motorcycle racer. In the 1970s he would become one of the best-known faces in British motorcycle racing. His regular tussles with Barry Sheene in Grands Prix and other events such as the World of Sport Superbike Challenge still make compelling viewing forty years later, and Grant is easily recognisable even on sometimes grainy footage, in his trademark green and white leathers and number ten.

In the early 1970s Grant began riding at the TT, on motorcycles prepared by his main sponsor Jim Lee, and by the middle of the decade he was riding Kawasaki factory machines. The Japanese company had started out manufacturing aircraft, and produced considerable numbers during the Second World War. Their interest in motorbikes developed much later, and it was not until the late 1960s that the Kawasaki Motorcycle Company began exporting significant numbers of machines. By the mid-1970s, Kawasaki UK were making a serious effort to raise their profile through racing, and Grant could see that they were on the verge of something really big. Over the next few years Kawasaki and Grant swept virtually all before them, taking scores of victories and breaking lap records throughout the British Isles. During this time the only serious challenge came from Barry Sheene and Suzuki GB, Kawasaki having left just about everyone else standing. Grant's first ride for the firm at the TT was in 1975, and in the Senior race that year he took an amazing victory in wet conditions. The engine seized on the first lap when,

Mick Grant in a Kawasaki jacket during the 1978 TT. (Courtesy of Ken Sprayson)

in the cold and damp air, the pistons expanded but the casings did not. He continued to coast, and the machine gradually warmed up and came back to life; shortly afterwards a pit board showed him that he was in fourth place! The engine continued to run without further trouble and on the last lap Grant really turned up the wick, setting the fastest lap and taking victory. Later that week, in the Classic TT, Grant, aboard a 750cc Kawasaki triple, shattered Mike Hailwood's outright lap record, which had stood for eight years, recording a speed of 109.82mph. Hailwood was watching in the commentary box and when he heard the news muttered, 'the bastard'. Grant took this as one of his greatest compliments. Despite the achievement he still lost the race, after his chain broke at Ballacraine.

In contrast, the 1976 TT was a forgettable experience. Despite a good showing in practice, in the Senior the 500cc engine seized, and in the 750cc Classic the clutch failed. In this era at the TT it was the Classic race that offered the big prize – £6000 – and in 1977 it attracted some big stars. Among the favourites were Suzuki rider John Williams, one of the biggest names in road-racing at the time, and Phil Read, who had returned to the TT after five years away. Grant was beset by chain problems once more. He was forced to nurse the bike round the last lap, but still won by a commanding margin. In the process he took back the outright lap record, which he had lost in 1976, being clocked at Creg ny Baa at an astonishing 191mph, a speed so fast that some questioned the accuracy of the recording equipment.

The 1978 Classic TT brought our next outstanding top twenty-five machine. The interest in this event had been building year on year and 1978 promised an outstanding field: the cream of late 1970s road-racing talent. John Williams was again on his Suzuki, Mike Hailwood (who had also returned to the TT) was on a factory-prepared Yamaha, and privateer Tom Herron (also on a Yamaha) had already won the Senior earlier in the week. A young Joey Dunlop, at only his second TT, also lined up on the grid. With them was Grant, on an updated version of the previous year's 750cc Kawasaki triple.

The KR750, as it was also known, was a water-cooled two-stroke, three-cylinder machine, first introduced in 1977 but improved upon for 1978. The in-line three-cylinder motor featured magnesium crankcases, rather than the more normal aluminium ones, which was was bending the rules slightly at the time, while the exhaust exited via two hand-crafted pipes on the left, and one on the right. With a race-standard right-foot gear-change, it achieved 128bhp at 9500rpm, though the power really started to kick in at about 6500rpm. Its biggest advantage over its main rivals was the fact that it was relatively light, giving a good power to weight ratio. As with all two-strokes, getting the jetting right was crucial. For the TT the carburettors would be set up at Jurby, which was close to sea level, but it was still a fine line between achieving maximum performance and seizing the engine. If the mechanics erred too much on the side of caution the machine would be sluggish on the mountain section, though some caution was necessary in order to actually finish a race; if the the jetting was too high, the machine had a tendency to seize at the end of Sulby Straight. The seven-spoke magnesium Morris wheels were originally fitted with twin front 296mm aluminium brake discs and a 235mm rear disc, but this was replaced by Kawasaki UK with cast-iron rear brakes, which were better suited to the British weather. Slick tyre technology was in its infancy in the mid-1970s and although Grant went out in the race with a slick on the rear, he still opted for a treaded tyre on the front. The riding position was pure 1970s. The rider sat low down, wedged between the high seat-back behind and the petrol tank in front. With his neat riding style, Grant tended to lean with the bike on corners and would not be seen hanging off or allowing his knee to skim the tarmac on bends in the style that Sheene had made so fashionable. Mick remembered:

> The Classic was billed as a showdown between Mike [Hailwood] and me and, though you generally ignore that sort of hype, I was as fascinated as anyone else by how we'd compare. At the time I had Brian Richards with a signal board at Laurel Bank, which allowed me to get my positions from the commentary post at Ballacraine (it later moved to Glen Helen). As I reached there on the first lap of the Classic, it read 'P1 +0' to Hailwood.[57]

It was, Grant observed ruefully, now becoming an interesting race. On the first lap, Hailwood and Grant were level on time. Hailwood had won the Formula 1 race earlier in the week aboard the Sports Motorcycles Ducati, and was hotly expected to win this outing as well, but his Yamaha was not in the same league as the Ducati. It lost a piston on that first lap, and he was forced to retire. The Yamaha of Tom Herron also developed mechanical problems, and he too fell by the wayside. Only Williams now presented a serious challenge to Grant, but his 500cc Suzuki RG500 was no match for the bigger-engined Kawasaki. On his second lap, Grant shattered the outright lap record once again, setting a blistering speed of 114.33mph. It was on the fourth lap, however, that the drama really began. As he approached Ballacraine, he became aware of a problem with the back brake. During practice week, Grant had had the engine remounted in the frame. As the motor was now held more firmly, there was more vibration than usual, and this eventually caused the brake master cylinder to work itself free of the chassis. As he braked coming into the sharp right-hander, Grant could feel the cylinder dangling by his left foot.

Mick Grant aboard the Kawasaki KR 750 triple in the 1978 Classic TT. This race was shaping up to be a thrilling showdown between Grant, the young pretender, and Mike Hailwood, the veteran. However, Hailwood's Yamaha soon expired. (Bikesport Fottofinders archives)

He believed that he could hold it safely with his boot, and prevent it from becoming entangled in the chain. As he later told a post-race press conference, he toyed with the idea of pulling into the pits, but feared that the scrutineers might not let him go out again if he did. The offending brake cylinder actually fell off at Parliament Square, but Grant raced on, leaving bemused marshals to pick it up from the road. Fortunately he was not black-flagged for having a dangerous machine. The real conundrum now was what to do about fuel. There was one more pit stop due, but Grant gambled on the fact that he would have enough in the tank to complete the final lap without pulling in. Mechanic Nigel Everett was ready at the grandstand, fully expecting the rider to come in, but Grant sailed past, remembering later:

Out of the corner of my eye, I could see Nigel stood trembling with this big fuel can and his mouth wide open as I went through flat out in fifth gear.

It was comical to see the vacant look on his face. After the race, we found there was a litre and a half left in the tank, which was a bit too close for comfort. I know there was a question of me being black-flagged and it had been reported around the circuit that something was dangling down, but I think common sense prevailed. No top rider... will do anything daft, and that includes me. Had I been black-flagged I think I might even have carried on, knowing it wasn't dangerous, and argued about it afterwards. It tickled me pink to get safely round at 112mph without a back brake. It won't be in the record books, but it pleased me to know I could tour round at 112mph in that state.[58]

As the race ended it was Grant first, followed by John Williams and Alex George. Sadly, this great TT win was to be the swansong for Grant's relationship with Kawasaki. The incident with the brake cylinder led to tensions with the team management, who were unhappy that Grant had modified the frame, and also implied that the failure was caused by one of his mechanics forgetting to screw the cylinder up tightly. Grant was dismayed to learn of this, commenting later:

I couldn't see why there had to be any questions asked. We'd done the job which was required, won the big race and set a new lap record as well. How it was achieved should not have mattered as long as it didn't involve cheating.[59]

Always the smallest of the Japanese manufacturers, the company's limited resources in terms of facilities and manpower, together with the distraction provided by the simultaneous development of the KR250/350 twin models, meant that the KR750 was never fully developed, and this was another reason for Grant's growing disillusion. The early success that Kawasaki had in 1975 had also discouraged them from putting in the effort required to stay on top in the following years. What had started out as a revolutionary and highly advanced machine was ultimately superceded, as rivals Suzuki and Yamaha regained their advantage. Grant went on to have more TT success with other marques, and the 750cc machine passed into the hands of former Kawasaki teammate Barry Ditchburn, who campaigned it in 1979. However, when Kawasaki allowed Ditchburn to keep it at the end of that season, Grant was able to buy it from him. He retains the 1978 Classic TT-winning Kawasaki as part of his personal collection, lovingly maintained and cared for. The machine is still in running order, although Mick imposes an 8500rpm rev limit on those few apart from himself whom he allows to ride it, in deference to the forty-year-old crank.

The 1978 Classic TT-winning machine lovingly cared for by Mick Grant as part of his personal collection. (Manx National Heritage)

The 1978 Classic was an amazing race, with an amazing rider and an amazing machine. The 1978 Grant Kawasaki 750 is an exceptionally rare beast, being one of only a handful built by the factory. It is also unquestionably one of the twenty-five greatest-ever TT motorcycles, and represents the pinnacle of Kawasaki's achievement at the TT in that decade. Aside from its TT performance, it is arguably among the greatest solo machines of the 1970s British racing scene, with a host of other competitive achievements to its name.

Chapter 16

500cc Suzuki RG 500 (rider Mike Hailwood) 1979

Suzuki's RG 500 is one of the most iconic machines in the history of motorcycle racing. A design classic in its own right, the four-cylinder engine perhaps represents the ultimate in two-stroke power. As one Suzuki designer put it, 'all we knew were two-strokes' so when in the early 1970s they wanted to design a new 500cc motor, it was natural for the company to simply upscale its smaller engines. It was introduced in 1974, and quickly came to dominate starting grids on racetracks around the world. As an off-the-peg racer it was affordable and highly effective, as Barry Sheene demonstrated by winning two 500cc world championships on Suzuki machinery in the 1970s. So when Mike Hailwood came to contest the 1979 TT (his final appearance at the event) there was one obvious piece of machinery on which to do it.

Hailwood's appearance at the 1978 TT after an absence of eleven years is still talked about today. To not only come back, but come back and win, riding bikes that were far more powerful than those he had raced in the 1960s, demonstrated just how great Hailwood's abilities really were. It was a testament to his character that he chose to do it at all, because he was already a legend, had nothing to prove, and indeed had everything to lose if it had all ended in embarrassing failure. At the time many observers, though they wished him well, secretly felt that he had little chance. As it was, his win in the Formula 1 TT on the Sports Motorcycles Ducati, prepared by Steve Wynne, has gone down in motorcycle racing history, and that machine (now held by the Ducati museum in Bologna) features in a previous chapter.

Hailwood's performance in other races at the 1978 TT, on the Martini Yamaha machines, was less impressive. Typically, Mike felt that he had not given his fans true value for money. So he chose to return to the TT in 1979 for a farewell appearance. This time he was a known quantity and his competitors knew that he would take some beating. They prepared accordingly, and Mike was going to need the best machinery he could lay his hands on if he was to be competitive. He and his long-time friend and mentor Ted Macauley first approached Yamaha, who had supplied the 1978 bikes, but (perhaps still smarting from that embarrassment) they replied that regrettably they did not have a machine available of the calibre that a rider of Hailwood's stature deserved. Of the other big manufacturers, only Suzuki felt confident enough to offer Hailwood a machine, and it was one of their Grand Prix standard RG500 bikes. Suzuki also agreed to send a full Grand Prix squad to the Isle of Man to support Mike. Led by race manager Rex White, the team comprised Gordon Whitehead, new mechanic Dave 'Radar' Cullen, and Martyn Ogbourne, who had prepared Barry Sheene's bikes. For Ogbourne it was a dream come true to be working for his boyhood hero, a man he reverentially referred to as 'God'.

Ogbourne, as chief mechanic for Suzuki GB, was in Japan (where he went each winter to liaise with the Suzuki factory technicians) when he learned by telex of Hailwood's tie-up with the British arm of the company. With the three 1979 factory-built machines already spoken for by Barry Sheene, Steve Parrish and Tom Herron, it was Ogbourne who built Hailwood's motorcycle (code named XR24) using whatever he could find. Although the frame was sound, it was still second-hand, having been used by Virginio Ferrari to win the West German Grand Prix the previous year. The engine had been salvaged from American rider Pat Hennen's machine from the 1978 TT. Hennen had suffered serious injuries when he came off in the Senior race, and although Hailwood was not superstitious, Macauley took a deliberate decision to conceal this information from him just in case. As well as the engine, the magnesium alloy wheels were also recovered from Hennen's machine, while the suspension units came from another spare frame left over from the 1978 season. By mid-February 1979, XR24 was ready for testing by Hailwood.

Mike had not been idle, and had sought advice on the quirks and foibles of the RG500 from Sheene and Parrish, who had apparently informed him that the type left a great deal to be desired in terms of handling. Hailwood met Sheene and Tom Herron at Heathrow airport after the 1979 Spanish Grand Prix, at which both had been thrown off. The two were bandaged and with a grey pallor about them, and it seemed to be further confirmation that the RG500 was a dangerous machine even in skilled hands. With this in mind, Hailwood approached the first testing session at Donington Park cautiously. He need not have worried. Within a couple of circuits he was cruising at speeds approaching the lap record. Returning to the pits, he was brimming with enthusiasm for the machine, telling Ogbourne, it was 'Great, just great. I like it very much indeed, and power... Jeez... there's tons of it.'[60]

Hailwood's main concern was that Ogbourne and his new colleague Cullen should fit a longer gear-change lever. Mike's leg had been damaged in a

Formula 1 car crash a few years earlier, and this would make things easier for him. Cullen and Ogbourne were somewhat taken aback:

> I could hardly believe what I was hearing. Nothing wrong with it! It was so unusual not to have some sort of criticism. But Mike is in a class of his own. Other men would have found something wrong with it just to get you geed up. Not Mike! And I didn't know what to do with myself. I'd expected to be working for the rest of the day – and was prepared to. But no! Mike told us to shove the bike in the van, lengthen the gear lever for his gammy foot, and fetch it to the Isle of Man.[61]

Before the Donington trial, the mechanics were somewhat skeptical that a veteran like Hailwood would be able to understand the myriad of suspension settings on a modern motorcycle. As Ogbourne remarked afterwards:

> Most of today's top-line riders have been able to get used to state-of-the-art suspension set-ups, and, with a little help, are able to cope with diagnosis and tuning. Hailwood [had] been virtually out of the saddle, apart from a couple of rides, since the old Honda days and might have been unable to interpret the signals fed back by the chassis during training.[62]

They need not have worried. Hailwood quickly understood the machine and, with both parties satisfied, the bike went off to be painted in his trademark racing colours of red, white and gold. Ogbourne had gained a reputation during his Grands Prix years with Sheene as a man with an eye for detail and nothing escaped him as he and Cullen prepared Hailwood's machine. The maestro could not have wished for more able assistants. Ogbourne in particular was quite simply the most experienced RG500 mechanic outside of the Hamamatsu factory, bringing with him insider knowledge of how, using a barometer, thermometer and a humidity meter, to prepare the factory carburettors, as well as how to set up the transmission, in which every gear ratio could be changed to suit a particular rider's style. During practice week things went well for Hailwood on the Suzuki, and he notched up the second-fastest speed in the early part of the week, 108.42mph. On the Friday night, the final practice session before Monday's Senior TT, it was widely hoped that he would post the fastest speed of the week. However, he pulled in after less than half a lap. When Ogbourne reached him, Hailwood told him that he thought a main bearing in the engine had failed, but the mechanic initially discounted this, believing instead that a carburation problem had developed. Ogbourne thought that he had set the two-stroke jets at too weak a mixture.

It was significant that the bike had stopped at one of the lowest points on the course, where on that cool Friday evening the air would be denser. It was common with two-strokes in this era for tuners to set the mixture slightly too weak, thus resulting in piston seizure. They retired to a garage in the grounds of the Majestic Hotel where the team was staying, and began the autopsy. Opening up the engine, the first warning sign was given by the partial seizure of Number 1 piston. When Ogbourne discovered that he could rattle the mainshaft of Number 1 crankshaft in its main bearing, he became resigned to the fact that there would be no sleep that night. Later, Hailwood called in to check on progress, and was assured that all was well despite the workshop being littered with motor parts, but Ogbourne recalled the look of dismay that the rider was unable to hide. It was obvious Hailwood feared that another humiliating debacle was about to unfold. Twenty-two hours later, at 8pm on the Saturday, the engine had been rebuilt, but when the mechanics fired it up, Number 1 cylinder was still pouring out clouds of acrid smoke. There was now only one day left before the Senior TT.

On Sunday morning, Ogbourne opened up the engine once more and carefully removed Number 1 crank. The smoke could only have come from gearbox oil reaching the crank case, either through a poor crank-case joint or a leaking crank oil seal. The crank-case faces looked good, which indicated a problem with the crank, so this had to be broken down into its components. The problem was traced to a faulty spring within it, a million to one failing, and now, with the dimly lit garage once again strewn with engine components, the rebuild could begin. Meanwhile, at short notice the ACU had changed its rules regarding standard fuel-fillers in the pit lane, allowing factory teams to use their own. Much Heath Robinson welding work took place in order to create a new custom-made fuel-filler, but a bigger problem was presented by the fuel tank on the RG500 itself. The one which the Suzuki team had brought to the Island was not large enough for Hailwood to operate a one pit-stop strategy, so a larger 40-litre tank was flown over during practice week. However, no one had realised that this tank was intended for the 1979 factory machines, which had subtly different frames. Wrongly positioned lugs on the new tank had to be hastily adjusted by an obscure aluminium welding factory in Castletown.

At 10pm on Sunday night, the engine was back in running order, and at 2am the team (minus Hailwood) carried out a pit-stop practice using real fuel. The 40-litre tank was filled in just nine seconds. By the time they had returned to the hotel, wired everything tight and given the machine a final polish, it was almost time to head back to the grandstand for scrutineering. With a race as arduous as the TT, Ogbourne had left nothing to chance. Even the rubber fairing mounts were lock-wired in place and reinforced with nylon tape, which would prevent the fairing from becoming detached if a mounting should shear. Ogbourne remembered afterwards that the events of the previous twenty-four hours had taken their toll on the Suzuki team:

> We were absolutely beat, we didn't get any sleep at all. Just time to snatch breakfast and get the bike up to the paddock. We certainly didn't feel on top form,and that's so vital when you've got to supervise one of those lightning fuel stops where every microsecond counts. But we expected Mike to be on a peak, so he had every right to expect us to be as well. The truth was that the bike we wheeled out for him had not been tried since we had built it up again; we just had to pray we had got it together okay. There was nothing else we could do.[63]

As it was, Hailwood's team worked together like clockwork. The pit-stop was so efficient that Hailwood, calmly wiping his visor with a cloth, actually appeared to be unready as the mechanics began pushing him back out.

Mike Hailwood at Union Mills in the 1979 Senior TT. Hailwood's neat tucked-in riding style is evident here as he powers the Suzuki RG 500 on. (Courtesy of Ken Sprayson)

The race itself, however, was fraught with difficulty. After taking it easy for the first lap to make sure that the bike was running well, Mike remembered:

> I'd hit the front when I came in for fuel, and that was done in double quick time by Martyn, even though he was bleary-eyed and weary. But I hadn't gone another two miles when I got one of those shocks that always seem to dog you at the TT... The bloody handlebars wouldn't let me turn acute right-hand bends. I didn't know it, but the damper had seized. I just knew I had a problem at the slower, sharper turns. It was okay on the fast bends, the longer swoops, but I had to heel it over and put my feet down to to tap-dance my way round on the acute corners... And there were three laps left, more than 100 miles. Luckily, I suppose, I was well ahead by then and I was able to knock it off a bit. I'd been giving the bike some stick earlier on, taking it up to ten-and-a-half thousand revs through the gears and eleven thou in top... about 180 miles an hour. But I knocked it back 500 and just tried to make sure I preserved the engine. Even then I got a fright, because it went onto three cylinders and kept cutting in and out all the way home on the last lap.[64]

Hailwood won by just over two minutes, and was wildly applauded as he came back up the return road. There were emotional scenes as fans tried to reach out to touch him or shake his hand as he returned to the grandstand. As he was heading towards the podium in the immediate aftermath of the race, an interviewer asked if, having raised the lap record to over 114mph, he had anything to say. A lesser man might have taken the opportunity to promote himself, but it was a mark of Hailwood's character that he replied, 'First of all, I'd like to thank my two mechanics, Martyn and Radar, who made it all possible by working on the bike throughout last night...'

Mike opted to use the Suzuki again in the final race of the week, the Schweppes Classic TT, but even though he took it to a 114.14mph lap and set a race average speed higher than he had achieved in the Senior, he was just unable to conquer Alex George's big 1000cc Honda. Despite what must have been a huge disappointment in narrowly missing out on a fifteenth TT win, Mike was as gracious as ever, telling reporters that he was pleased to have come in behind George, as he'd never had a second place on the Isle of Man before.

A few weeks after that historic final TT, Suzuki presented the machine to Mike as a memento. After many years as part of the Donington Collection, Hailwood's RG500 is now permanently preserved at the Manx Museum in Douglas, after it was purchased at a sale of Hailwood family memorabilia in 1997. It makes the top twenty-five machines with ease, and it has been described by one expert

Hailwood celebrates victory after the 1979 Senior. (Courtesy of Ken Sprayson)

as being in the top ten surviving historic British racing motorcycles, alongside the Barry Sheene Grands Prix bikes. However, controversy has surrounded the machine for many years, with a persistent rumour current among some TT fans that it is either a replica, or a machine supplied for use in the 1979 Dutch TT, which Hailwood never used. On balance it would seem that several pieces of evidence prove the conspiracy theorists to be wrong. Firstly, Mike's friend Ted Macauley has confirmed in conversation with the author that Mike would never have accepted a replica. Secondly, careful study pays rewards. Comparison with photos from 1979 reveals some twelve points of congruity between the machine in the Manx Museum and the bike Mike was riding on the Island in 1979. These include details such as the brakes, clocks, position of stickers on the frame, exhausts and other apparently trivial items, all of which tally. If it is a replica, then it is an astonishingly good one, and why would Suzuki GB go to the trouble of creating a pastiche when it would be far easier just to give Mike the real thing? It was almost three years out of date as a racing machine and of little value to them.

The poster produced by Hailwood to accompany the RG500 at a bike show in 1980. 113.03mph is the machine's race average speed from the Classic TT, in which Hailwood came second, actually higher than in the Senior, which he won. (Manx National Heritage)

Another important clue came from the Hailwood family archive in 2014, when a poster was found among Mike's photo albums, which he had produced in 1980 to display alongside the bike at a motorcycle show. It states unequivocally 'Suzuki RG500 Senior TT winner'. It is inconceivable that a man of Mike's integrity would make such a claim for anything other than the real machine, and he would certainly have known if it was not. Perhaps the most crucial piece of evidence, however, is the motorbike itself. Close examination of the Suzuki's internals reveals a liberal scattering of code stamps on the engine components. All contain the letters XR 22. The XR 22 code was only applied to the 1978 factory machines (the 1976–77 machines were XR 14s and the 1979 factory machines were all XR 27s). The fact that the machine in the Manx Museum has this code proves that the engine was a 1978 model; furthermore, Suzuki GB had access to only two such machines in 1978. One was used by Pat Hennen and the other was raced by Barry Sheene. Sheene's 1978 bike was part of his personal collection in Australia, so the only source for this engine *must* be the damaged Hennen machine, as Ted Macauley knew. The fact that the Hailwood machine is an XR 22 is corroborated by Ray Battersby in his definitive book *Team Suzuki*. Battersby adds another crucial piece of detail by providing the frame number for Barry Sheene's 1978 machine, only two digits away from the one on the Hailwood bike, thereby confirming the date of the latter.

The 1979 Suzuki RG500 as it appears today. (Manx National Heritage)

The machine is made all the more poignant by Mike's tragic and pointless death, with his daughter, in a road accident caused by a careless lorry driver just two years later. While others have come along who might claim to have equalled or exceeded his talent, few can match him in terms of warmth, charisma and popularity. More than anything else, the Hailwood RG500 stands as a fitting memorial to a man who put far more into the TT than he ever took out of it.

Chapter 17

750cc Windle Yamaha sidecar outfit (rider Jock Taylor/Benga Johansson) 1980

Even today, more than thirty years after his death, many TT fans and competitors regard 1980 world champion Jock Taylor as the greatest ever sidecar racer. In this chapter, we examine what is unquestionably the Scottish competitor's most significant Isle of Man machine, aboard which he and passenger Benga Johansson won four races and set two new sidecar lap records. So impressive was their performance at the 1982 TT, that the record they set was one that many people, at the time and afterwards, believed would never be beaten. Indeed, some older sidecar racers, who competed at the TT in the 1970s, would argue that the changes to the course have been so great that Jock's record never *can* be beaten.

John Robert 'Jock' Taylor was born in Pencaitland, near Edinburgh, and began racing in 1974 aged nineteen, as a sidecar passenger. By 1975 he was in the driving position, with an ex-Mac Hobson BSA twin. Like many other British champions he earned his spurs the hard way, struggling in his early club events with no financial backing. In those early years he made do with worn tyres, tired engines and race fuel that was in short supply. One observer remembered that he would travel down to North Gloucester club meetings at Gaydon in Warwickshire. He used an old bus as a transporter and when it arrived at the trackside, out would pour a whole gang of faithful Scottish supporters. So loyal were these early fans that they even clubbed together to pay for the petrol to enable Taylor to get down to the meeting.

By 1977, Taylor had switched to Yamaha machinery and was starting to make a mark at British level, his most significant achievement being the setting of a new lap record of over 105mph at the Ulster Grand Prix. In the same year he won the Scottish Championship and came second in the British Championship with fellow Scot Lewis Ward in the chair. Together the two scored an eye-catching win at Oulton Park in Cheshire, and this brought Taylor to the attention of a major sponsor in the form of Fowlers of Bristol, one of the biggest motorcycle dealers in south-west England. In the 1978 season they backed him for a first attempt at the world championship series. Despite Ward quitting midway through the year, with Fowlers' support Taylor put together a very creditable first season, with a third place in his home event, the British Grand Prix, fourth place in Czechoslovakia, sixth in Belgium, seventh in France and eighth in Italy, giving him an overall finish of seventh place.

The highlight of the 1978 season, however, was the Isle of Man TT, where with Kenny Arthur in the chair Jock finished second and third in the two sidecar legs, setting a new lap record of 101.22mph in the process. In 1979 a winning pairing was born when, finding himself without a passenger for the Snetterton Race of Aces event, Jock appealed over the circuit tannoy for someone to come forward. From out of the solo paddock came a young Swede who had so far enjoyed only modest success – twenty-two-year-old Bengt-Goran (Benga) Johansson. After completing his two years of national service in the Swedish army, Johansson (who was the son of a stock car racer from Ljungby near Anderstorp) rode a Morbidelli to second place in the Swedish championship, but struggled to break into the Grand Prix circuit and sold the machine. Having tried his luck at UK meetings he had again achieved only patchy success. His interest in sidecars was slight until that day when he answered Taylor's appeal, but the two clicked right away and became a pairing for the remainder of Taylor's career. With Johansson on board he took his maiden Grand Prix win just a few weeks after meeting him for the first time, appropriately enough in front of the passenger's home fans in Sweden. Up to that point, Taylor had been using a hub-centred Seymaz chassis, but later that year he acquired from Terry Windle a short wheelbase outfit. It was on this machine that Taylor would enjoy so much success, both on and off the Isle of Man.

By 1980 the Scottish/Swedish pairing was poised for an all-out assault on the world title. Fowlers' racing boss, renowned engine-builder Dennis Trollope, had put together no fewer than fifteen 500cc Yamaha engines on which to carry the world campaign, along with a further selection of 750cc motors for use in international meetings like the Isle of Man TT. With other financial backing in place as well, this meant that all Taylor had to supply was his riding talent. He took victory at the Dutch TT, and the Belgian and Finnish Grands Prix, so that by the time he reached the British Grand Prix at Silverstone in August that year, the title was within his reach. Despite two of his main rivals dropping out with mechanical troubles, the race was still full of drama, with Taylor and Johansson suffering a slow puncture that cost them first place. Finishing second, however, was enough to hand them the world title. The same season had seen them raise the bar again at the TT, on the Windle chassis. Johansson had only seen the TT course for the first time in January of that year, and after an intense return visit in May in which he crammed in fifteen laps in a car, he felt that he knew the layout sufficiently well. In practice week his course knowledge grew further and he began to feel more and more comfortable with the Mountain circuit. His only difficulties, he recalled later, came from the bumpy surface (despite having fitted extra padding to the sidecar platform in order to try to compensate) and the glare of the setting sun during evening practice sessions. After battling to second place in wet conditions during the first race, they won the Sidecar B event convincingly and chopped twenty-eight seconds off the lap record in the process, taking it to 106.08mph.

In 1981 Taylor retained his British title and claimed further laurels in the TT, taking his tally of wins there to three. After wearing out two engines during practice week, they went into the first race with a brand-new 700cc engine built the night before by Dennis Trollope. Described by *Motor Cycle News* as

Jock Taylor and Benga Johansson after victory in the second 1981 sidecar TT race. A pleased Dennis Trollope stands behind. (Courtesy of Ken Sprayson)

'the world's most exciting sidecar partnership,' the two set off at a blistering pace and took an astonishing 24.2 seconds off their record lap time from the previous year. It was a close-run thing, as they finished the race with only fumes in the fuel tank, with Taylor explaining afterwards:

> We'd planned to stop for one or two gallons. But when it started to rain around Black Hut on the Mountain on the second lap I decided the extra petrol would be unnecessary.[65]

As the tail-enders completed their last lap, there was a real cloudburst, but it was too late to really slow the leaders down. Johansson added afterwards:

> Coming from the GPs, it was completely different. There was no scratching at all. It was damp in Ramsey so we had to go carefully. I thought we'd do 103 or 105. I was really surprised we went round at 108 mph.[66]

In the second sidecar race that year, the duo showed how far ahead of the rest of the field they were. In spite of mechanical problems, which meant their speed was considerably down on the first outing, they still beat second-place man Dick Greasley by nearly two minutes. They had started off slowly in order to try to preserve the Yamaha motor, and were hoping to complete the three laps without stopping for fuel. Only if they were seriously pressed and forced to thrash the engine would they have to come into the pits. At first they were trailing main rival Trevor Ireson. However, after Ballaugh Bridge they were in the lead by five seconds, even though they had experienced a major slide at the thirteenth milestone, after which Taylor slackened off again. The real drama began on the mountain climb on the second lap when the fuel pump gave out, and they had to hand pump petrol to the engine. Yet it was still a commanding victory.

It was 1982 that brought Taylor and Johansson's greatest achievement at the Isle of Man TT. It was, however, a disappointing story in the first sidecar race when, despite being favourites, the duo hit big problems on the first lap. Taylor was distracted by the temperature gauge, and they clipped a bank. They eventually finished eighteenth, while Mick Boddice, who led for two laps, was forced to retire on the final lap with engine failure. Trevor Ireson (with passenger Donnie Williams) moved to the top of the leader board and had no such worries, taking the chequered flag in front of Greasley and Hanks.

Boddice's bad luck continued in the second race, which took place in glorious conditions. He led Taylor by a fraction of a second when he was forced out at Sulby Crossroads on the second lap. Taylor was cruising initially, as he needed to run in his Yamaha engine following an all-night repair job to fix a broken cylinder-head stud, but turned up the wick to put himself four seconds ahead at the half-way point. With the departure of Boddice, Taylor took over control of the race, and even though he stopped for fuel at the end of lap two he still managed to shave two seconds off his lap record from the previous year. In the final blistering circuit he increased the lap record to 108.29mph, to win from husband and wife team Dennis and Julia Bingham, and Steve Abbott with Shaun Smith in third. Overall victory from the two races went to Roy Hanks and Vince Biggs, who were fifth in that second race, but Taylor's lap record was an astonishing achievement. Some measure of this can be gained from the fact that it stood unbroken for seven years. Indeed, there were some who said it would never be broken, and as the years rolled on, changes to the course (particularly to smooth out Sulby Straight, which at that time was like riding on corrugated iron, and to Quarry Bends, which after road alterations became a gear faster) meant that it never could be beaten. Taylor himself put his astonishing speed down to the fact that this time round he had moved the temperature gauge, so that it was now Johansson's responsibility to watch it!

Taylor and Johansson with the Windle outfit at Braddan Bridge, in the 1982 sidecar TT second race. (Bikesport Fottofinders archives)

Just weeks after their achievement in the TT, Taylor and Johansson travelled to take part in the Finnish Grand Prix. Taylor had been developing a long wheelbase machine to compete in world championships, and although he did not like it due to a tendency to leap across the road, he had decided to persevere with it. The four-times TT winning short wheelbase machine was left at home, prepared in readiness for the forthcoming British championship round at Donington. On race day at the Finnish circuit at Imatra, like the TT also a closed roads course, the heavens opened. Jock was the sidecar riders' representative and gave the go-ahead for the sidecar Grand Prix to take place. It was a decision that would have fatal consequences. In the rain-soaked conditions, Taylor and Johansson's outfit aquaplaned and slid off at a corner, colliding with a telegraph pole as it did so. Taylor survived the initial impact, but as he was receiving attention from marshals at the scene another outfit (piloted by a Finnish rider) suffered a similar misfortune and slid off at the same place. It collided with the wreckage of Taylor's outfit and the race was red-flagged as medics attended the injured. Jock died that evening from the injuries sustained in the second crash. His family and friends learned of his death via a BBC sports broadcast that night.

Jock's world championship-winning sidecar, with which he also set the TT 108.29mph lap record, remained in the hands of his financial backer Dennis Trollope, but another long-time sponsor, Tom Wheatcroft, owner of the Donington Park racing circuit, asked if it could be put on display in his museum. The Donington Collection held a number of important machines, including a Jackie Stewart Formula One car, and Trollope had no hesitation in agreeing. There it remained for twenty-six years. After Wheatcroft's death, the Donington museum was dismantled and Trollope was asked to take the machine back. Unfortunately, during the last few years at Donington after Wheatcroft passed away, there were a number of thefts from the bike. Parts of the bodywork and stickers were removed, but most significantly the Lectron carbs, with which Jock Taylor had enjoyed so much success, and which had been given to him by his friend Kenny Roberts (500cc solo world champion in 1978) were taken and never recovered. Dennis Trollope was not immediately able to remove the Taylor machine, so welcomed an offer from a five-man consortium who offered to buy the outfit. Part of the deal was that these individuals would restore the bike to its original condition and display it in a museum in Alford, Aberdeenshire. However, for cost reasons this never happened, and for four years it lay in Alford in pieces in a shed.

At a race meeting, Scottish sidecar world championship competitor Stuart Muldoon bumped into Dennis Trollope and enquired after the Taylor bike (Jock Taylor having been his boyhood hero). Upon being told of its fate, he phoned his father, Jack Muldoon, Jock's friend and fellow competitor from the 1970s. Immediately an offer was made by the Muldoons to acquire the machine, which was soon accepted. The family bought Jock's bike in March 2012, but it was in a sorry state. Jack Muldoon recalls his anger at the way Jock's machine had been neglected in the years since it left Donington:

> ...the bike was lying in bits the engine half stripped, bits of it were everywhere lying in amongst dirt, rats' shit, and straw... all the parts of the bike and bodywork were laying in the dirt... we loaded the bike and all that went with it into the van, then Dennis told me how much money he wanted for the bike, I paid him in cash that I had brought up with me in a briefcase.[67]

Muldoon started the restoration work immediately. The sidecar was to be completely stripped to a bare chassis, and months were spent with emery paper cleaning and polishing it. In the twenty-six years that it had been housed at Donington in the museum, and then in the four years up in Aberdeen, the chassis and all components had become covered in rust and everything was seized; every component on the bike needed to be stripped and cleaned, all bearings in the chassis needed to be replaced, and the engine completely rebuilt. This was done with the help of Bill Howarth and Dennis Trollope, who supplied all the Yamaha TZ700 parts required in the engine rebuild. Other help came from Terry Windle, Stuart Mellor and Paul Drake. Jack Muldoon continues his account, with a sense of awe at what he had acquired:

> We arrived back from Alford on Saturday tea time, and immediately unloaded Jock's bike into my workshop... on the Sunday morning my grandson and I went into the workshop to start the restoration of the most famous sidecar in the world and the history of sidecar racing. I had the 1980 Windle TZ 700 Taylor/Johansson world championship and TT lap record winning sidecar in my possession, and now had the privilege of restoring it to what it was in 1980. Our first duty was to take an inventory and photographs of all we had received with Jock's package; we started with all the items that were in boxes: mechanical parts/ paperwork/clothing items, i.e. original NEW 36-year-old T shirts still in their cellophane bags, unopened. 1980, 36-year-old posters, stickers, and all parts that the consortium had removed from the sidecar: nuts, bolts, jubilee clips, brackets, throttle cables, throttle and clutch lever and clutch cable. Dennis had pointed out to me these three items and told me these were given to Jock from Kenny Roberts 500cc world champion, they

are genuine Yamaha factory parts and if damaged, cannot be replaced. They were lying in a box with the clutch basket on top of them when we retrieved the bike from Alford.

After carrying out the inventory of all the mechanical parts that we had they were washed off in our parts washer, cleaned, dried, labelled, photographed then boxed and put away. We then lifted Jock's bike up onto stands, and started the strip down; the first thing was again to photograph the bike as complete as it was, as the consortium had removed parts of the engine. The first thing we removed was the brake calipers then its wheels, all the brake lines, brake master cylinders, passenger floor, and then the famous 108.29mph TT lap TZ700 engine. It was placed in an engine stand I had made many years ago... I was more than glad that I had not disposed of it. [I also had] a clutch plate removal tool we had made, and various other tools we made for the TZ engines, ignition timing disc, stator and rotor removing tool, gudgeon pin removing tool and others...

We then removed all other items till we were left with the bare chassis; our next step was to remove the front Koni shock absorbers, forks, rear shocker and swinging arm, all the individual parts that we removed were laid out on our benches, and again photographed and labelled ready for cleaning. Next job was to remove all bearings from all components, i.e. head stock, swinging arm, wheels, and rear hub, inventory the numbers from the bearings and replace, keeping in mind that all these items on Jock's bike were 36 years old.

Now we had in front of us the completely bare chassis, our first priority was to refurbish this part; this was in the hands of my grandson Steven. Chassis and all chassis components, exhausts, wheels, water expansion tank, fuel tank, anything that had to be cleaned with 1000 grit Emery and polished with Ultimate Alloy Cleaner was Steven's job. I concentrated on the mechanical side but with help from Steven, we had to be very careful not to go over the top with the polishing, it had to be as original as it was when Jock/Benga rode it for the first time in 1980. It took us 4/5 months on the cleaning/polishing side of the restoration, when that was complete we went over it with magnifying glasses and Ultra Violet lights to see if there were any metal cracks in the chassis, chassis components & wheels, [but] all was excellent. I had difficulty finding the same type of bearings that Terry Windle used when building the chassis in 1980, but I contacted BJ Bearings in Cumbernauld near Glasgow and told them what I was after. Lo and behold the parts manager was a biker and a fan back then of Jock's, within a week

I had all the bearings and more, made by Timken Bearings, that were equivalent to the numbers I had asked for, I contacted Koni Shocks via Redline Suspension, who told me to send all the shocks down for them to see their condition, as they were now 35 years old.[68]

Muldoon contacted all the parts manufacturers who had sponsored Jock, and whose items were used on his chassis, including AP Lockheed, who supplied brake calipers, HEL Performance for brake hoses, Questmead for brake pads, Raceline Suspension who supplied Koni shock absorbers, Silkolene Oils, Dunlop Tyres, Martek Composite who supplied the fairings, Bill Howarth and Dennis Trollope for TZ Spares, and Dave Cheesemond for wheels and brake discs. He told them that he now owned Jock's outfit, and had started a complete restoration, and asked if they could help him in any way. AP Lockheed fully refurbished the five calipers and three master cylinders, retaining Jock's original calipers, pistons, and master cylinders. Questmead asked Mintex to make and supply the brake pads with the original friction material they were made of in 1982. HEL Brake Hoses asked him to label each hose and send them down, then made up all new brake hoses exactly like Jock's. They used the banjo fitting end from Jock's hoses, and put them into the new ones so as to keep their originality. Although they felt that after the bike had been static for thirty-five years, for safety reasons it was necessary to replace all of the hoses, they also returned the original hoses to Muldoon. Redline Suspension asked for all of the shockers to be sent to them complete; they then stripped them all down to just casings, assessed what was required, then rebuilt all the shocks. They made all new internals, seals and pressure valves for them, and Muldoon got them back with the original casings and springs unpainted the way he sent them, again in order to keep their originality. He contacted Dave Cheesemond, and asked if he could make a set of three wheels for wet tyres to go on, as well as checking over the original wheels. Cheesemond did this, and sent the original wheels to a friend of his who put them in a lathe and spun and polished them. They then appeared brand new. He also made four new brake discs for the machine, again for safety reasons.

Jock is believed to have been the only rider ever to have two oil companies sponsor him at the same time – Castrol for the world championships and Silkoline for the TT, so Muldoon contacted Silkoline Oils, and spoke to the manager there. He sent up a pallet of oils, lubricants, brake fluids, grease, polish and contact cleaners. Dunlop Tyres, who had been Taylor's tyre sponsor thirty-five years previously, had stopped making sidecar tyres, and the formats used had all been scrapped. Nonetheless they got in touch with Yokohama, who on the recommendation of Dunlop supplied Muldoon with six slick and wet tyres, asking only if he would keep the Dunlop stickers on the bike, which was done. Next Muldoon contacted Stuart Mellor of Martek Composites, who made the fairings for Jock's bike. He told Mellor the whole story, and asked if he could make a set of fairings as near as possible to the original ones that are on the bike. He wanted a spare set so that any racing or parade use would not put further damage on the original ones, as they still carry the flies and stone chips from the outfit's last TT, and are the ones that were on when it won the 1980 world championship and posted the 108.28 TT lap record. Mellor instead offered to go one better, revealing that he still had the original mould that Jock's fairings had come out of. A second set from this mould was duly produced and mounted on the machine. The only change that had to be made was to widen the seat, as Jock was skinnier than most riders today! It was done very professionally and was not obvious. Jack flattened all the bodywork with 800 grit rubbing down paper, drilled the front air holes for the discs carefully as they had to look original, made the wire mesh pattern for the front radiator grill and fitted it. Then the bodywork was primed, and flattened again with 1000 grit. It was time now to put on the first colour (blue) then the second colour (white), two coats of each colour then the same with the side stripes in red and gold, again two coats, then a coat of lacquer over all the painted bodywork. Lining it off was quite a task as it was not painted straight on the original, but these fairings had to look as close as possible to the real thing. Next came the sponsors' vinyls. All were over thirty-six years old and could no longer be found. However, Jack's nephew Chris Gusman, a graphic designer, had the answer. He came down to the garage, took photos, measured all the lettering on the original fairings, and made new lettering and stickers identical to those on Jock's original, then lettered the new fairings. The original fairings are now at the village of Pencaitland where Jock was born, on display in ex-sidecar driver Willie Stewart's private museum. Here they reside along with the original three Dunlop tyres that were on the outfit when Muldoon got it, as used at Jock's last TT in 1982.

The new Yokohama tyres were fitted to the new wheels by Express Tyres at Lockerbie, as a favour by Ian Hamilton, whose father Sam was also a friend and fellow competitor of Jock's. Massive help was also given in locating TZ spares for Jock's engine by Dennis Trollope, Bill Howarth, Dave Holden and Steve Webster MBE, ten times world champion, for whom Jock was a boyhood hero. Astonishingly, when asked what they were owed, every single one of the above-mentioned manufacturing companies and individuals answered in the same vein. All asked for nothing, seeing it as their contribution to the restoration of the greatest and most famous sidecar outfit in the world. All were proud and honoured to help, in memory of Jock Taylor, a breathtaking illustration of the affection in which he is still held. With all the mechanical components at the various manufacturers, Jack Muldoon began the refurbishment of the engine. He said:

I raced these thoroughbreds myself and have built dozens of them. I plugged up all holes and ports then steam cleaned it to remove all oil and grease from the engine, it was thirty-five years' worth of dirt. I photographed the engine before stripping it down. When we collected the outfit from up in Alford, the left-hand cylinders and head had been removed and the cases were showing the cranks. They were uncovered and full of dirt and bits of straw. I removed the other cylinders and head, I washed the parts in the parts washer and photographed all, and I then measured the port heights using a digital micrometer. Ex port heights were taller than standard G cylinders which would explain its top end power, as it is very fierce from mid range upwards, and In ports measured wider, possibly to match the works 38mm Lectron carbs that were on it. I also measured the cylinder-head squish clearance area, it was also deeper than any TZ heads I run. It was a very interesting top end. I was told from the horse's mouth that he ran very large Mains and PJ sizes, I checked the ignition timing before I stripped the right-hand cylinders off and he was running very advanced settings, which may explain the big jets, [however] I will not divulge any of the measurements from the internals of Jock's engine, nor the timing settings.

I then removed the ignition rotor and stator, clutch basket, casing lock plate and all casing bolts, I split the casings and removed the cranks and gearbox. I called Dennis Trollope and asked him how old the gearbox was, as on close inspection there appeared to be no wear on the shims or meshing gear dogs. He told me it was a new gearbox that was fitted as Jock was to be racing at the British Championship at Donington on his return from Imatra, [and] it was all prepared for that forthcoming meeting. I measured all the gearbox parts as a matter of course, I then thoroughly inspected the crank casings for any cracks or hidden fractures, as the TZ engines were prone to throwing rods. I had them examined under ultra violet light, but all was OK there. As the cranks were thirty-five-plus years old and had never been turned over while it lay at Donington, I split the cranks and had all new rod kits, main bearings and small end bushes, Labyrinth Seals and crank seals all replaced. I weighed the four pistons that were in the engine and all were the same. Number 3 cylinder had some light scoring on the Ex side of it, as did the piston. I cleaned the cylinder with acid and replaced the four pistons and rings with new ones.[69]

Jack then removed all other parts from the crank casings, the water pump and water pump transfer tube and O-rings. The crank casings were steam-cleaned, dried and all components refurbished and installed. The gearbox was rebuilt, measured and refitted, the cranks were installed next and then synchronized with the final drive gear, with crank timing marks flush with the casing face. The crank end float was again checked and measured, the clutch selector rod was fitted and top casing offered to bottom casing. It fitted perfectly, so the crank cases were bolted down and tightened to the correct torque. The water pump tube was fitted, as was the water pump elbow. After the sump was fitted, the engine was placed into the bench cradle for top-end assembly. New base gaskets and paper gaskets were measured and fitted, the cylinders were jacked up to correct port heights, pistons were installed and rings were chamfered and gapped. The cylinders and heads were fitted and the tops of the pistons were smeared at the edges with grease, and water volumed. Next the heads were removed, grease was cleaned out and the heads were put back on. New NGK sparkplugs were put in to stop any foreign bodies from dropping down the plug holes, while the cylinder heads were tightened to the correct torque. Carburettor rubbers were fitted to the cylinders, plugs were removed and clock gauges fitted, ignition stator and rotor fitted and ignition timing carried out. The clutch basket was fitted and plates installed, then the engine rebuild was complete and the engine was wrapped up and put away.

It was now time to turn back to the chassis. All the new bearings that had to be fitted to it (for head stock, swinging arm and so on) were done, and assembly of all the parts could now begin. Firstly the rear swinging arm, front forks and all calipers were refitted. Next came the routing of the all the brake hoses back to where they were at the time of stripping. At this point all the early photographs taken before removal came into their own. All brake lines were put in and clipped, ready to attach banjo ends onto the calipers. The front mudguard was attached, as was the front handlebar master cylinder. The clutch lever was fitted, followed by rear brake master cylinders and rear brake pedal, then front and rear shockers. Next came the rear hub and rear sprocket. Before the passenger floor could be fitted a new one had to be made, as the old one was contaminated with thirty-five years of oil and fuel and was rotten, but the original floor brackets were used.

Now the rebuilt TZ700 engine was installed, and refurbished exhausts fitted, as were new springs. New discs were fitted to the refurbished Windle wheels, then the wheels themselves were fitted and calipers reattached along with new brake pads. Brake pipes were fitted to the calipers and the system bled. All water hoses and header tank were now attached, and the water system also bled. Then the steering damper and fuel tank were installed. Jack remembered:

> We were just about ready to fire it up, only 500ml of gearbox oil needed to go in and then it came down off the stands... after [that] we put fuel in the tank with a lot of oil mix as the engine had never been fired up since I rebuilt it, so I wanted to put plenty of lubricant around all the internals i.e. pistons, main bearings and cylinders, plus this was the first time in 36 years it had been fired up, the last person to have fired it up was Jock Taylor himself, so this was going to be a bit emotional. We pushed it up to the top of my driveway at the house, selected first gear, lifted the clutch, put the chokes on, put the fuel pump on and pushed it down the driveway, after 20 feet dumped the clutch and it fired up on all four straight away. I revved it several times to clear the oil from the exhausts, took it out of gear put the chock under the front wheel and proceeded to warm it up, no water leaks from the radiator or hoses, seals all good. I warmed it up blipping it to 5000rpm for ten minutes then to 10000 for another ten minutes till she was at her correct temperature. I had a lot of tears in my eyes, I looked up to the sky and said to Jock, thank you, his love child was making proper noises again. The only problem was that when you took it off the chokes it struggled to rev, so it went back up on the stands and I checked fuel pressure, ignition timing, fuel pumps, but could not find any problems with the above.[70]

A few weeks later, in August 2012, the restoration was 90 per cent complete. Jack took the machine to the Jock Taylor Memorial Meeting at East Fortune near Edinburgh, a few miles from where Jock was born and brought up. As well as displaying the outfit in front of members of Jock's family for the first time – an emotional event for all concerned – he was able to discuss the engine problem with Jock's old mechanic, Pete Novak. Also present was former Scottish champion Alan Duffus:

> When we collected the sidecar at Alford, Dennis Trollope gave me four old Lectrons, which... were found to be no use. I then bought a set of second-hand Lectrons from the USA and paid £3,000 for them, [but] while awaiting the arrival of the carbs, Alan Duffus of Alan Duffus Yamaha Motorcycles, Kirkaldy approached me and said, 'Will it not rev without the chokes on?' I replied no, he said come through to my shop tomorrow and I'll give you a brand new set of the same Lectrons, to try on it, if it cures the problem keep them. He had them for a TZ750 twenty years ago, tried them once and took them back off, he said the power delivery was too fierce for

Back on the Isle of Man once more, Stuart Muldoon prepares to take the Jock Taylor Windle outfit out on the parade lap, June 2013. (Courtesy of Jack Muldoon)

his TZ. I asked him how much did he want for them, he said NOTHING that's my contribution to the restoration of Jock's bike, as he was a good friend of his. I went through next morning, got the carbs, fitted them that night and fired it up. Problem cured, we were now rocking and rolling.[71]

Appropriately, Stuart Muldoon, ex-TT Rider, and the only other sidecar driver from Scotland apart from Jock Taylor to have won a Grand Prix, together with his passenger and cousin Chris Gusman, was the first to ride Jock's bike again after its restoration, for a lap round the TT course in 2013. After so much work, Jack found that it brought a lump to his throat to have the machine back at the scene of so much past glory:

When we were asked to bring Jock's bike over to the IOM to do the demo lap it was Stuart and Chris that rode it, it was the first time in 36 years Jock's bike was again going down Bray Hill, it was emotional, and I felt very proud of what we had achieved, by doing it we have kept Jock's memory alive. Myself and my old passenger Donald Kay were asked back that same year to the Manx to do another demo lap. Special thanks to Paul Philips and Bruce Baker and all their staff at the IOM TT who organised everything to have the Jock Taylor bike there, I can never thank them enough for what they did.[72]

So machine number seventeen in our greatest twenty-five has risen like a phoenix from the ashes, and the amazing story of its return from dereliction to working and running outfit is as intriguing as that of its incredibly talented rider. It is also a fitting tribute to its his meteoric rise to racing stardom. Few other machines can claim four TT wins, two TT lap records, a world championship and a host of other victories. A truly astonishing outfit, it is now kept in a private museum in Scotland.

Chapter 18

Yamaha OWO1 750cc (rider Carl Fogarty) 1992

Yamaha's FZR750R OWO1 is one of the most distinctive racing machines ever designed. The street version was first shown to the public at the Earl's Court motorcycle show in October 1988, and in racing trim it went on to take the two-wheeled world by storm, winning races at club, British Superbike and World Superbike levels. The bike was Yamaha's first real attempt to take the World Superbike championship, and was designed in direct response to Honda's dominant RC30 machine. The OWO1 was a motorcycle ahead of its time in many ways, but a serious price tag put it out of reach of many racers, and it is estimated that only around 110 racing machines were sold in the UK between 1989 and 1992. One of these rare beasts is our next greatest TT machine – the motorbike on which Carl Fogarty fought his epic battle with Steve Hislop in 1992, a story which in itself is a major part of the legend of the TT.

First it is necessary to examine the pedigree of this awesome machine in more detail. It is fair to say that Yamaha had a particularly fine superbike in the street-going FZR750R. Producing over 100bhp just in its road trim, the FZ was right alongside the fastest sports bikes of its day. The design featured a revolutionary five-valve cylinder head and cleverly placed the alternator behind the inclined cylinder block, which resulted in a motor which for its day was extremely narrow. A six-speed gearbox meant that the four-stroke, four-cylinder engine could be kept absolutely on the boil and placed the bike comfortably for conversion to a racing machine. In fact, the reason it was so easy to convert to a racing bike is that basically, that was what it was. In order to comply with World Superbike rules, Yamaha had to produce for sale at least 1,000 of the road-going version of their racing machine. As the company's vision was firmly on the racing scene, little attention was given to rider comfort or other luxuries on the road bike. If you wanted to race one, it was basically a case of removing the number plate, lights and tax disc holder.

As good as the FZR750R was, the factory racing version, with identification code OWO1, was at a different level. The alloy delta box-beam frame was developed from the FZR but was thinner, lighter and reportedly of much better material than on the road bikes. The front suspension, with 43mm fork legs, was upgraded with a full range of adjustment. The rear was even more improved, with a full-spec Ohlins race unit featuring a remote hydraulic pre-load adjuster. If the chassis was good, the 749cc four-cylinder motor was outstanding. Yamaha retained the twenty-valve (three inlet and two exhaust) layout of the FZR motor, but refined it with titanium connecting rods, lightweight pistons, EXUP butterfly valves in the exhaust and a close ratio, six-speed gearbox. Feeding the engine were 38mm flat-side Mikuni carburettors.

Despite the EXUP valves to aid mid-range power, riders were expected to keep the OWO1 above 9,000rpm, and a mighty 119bhp was available at 14,000rpm. The bike was littered with titanium and carbon fibre parts and weighed in, complete with road equipment, at a very competitive 412 pounds plus fuel and oil. Despite Yamaha's best efforts at making the bike lighter, the OWO1 was still a big motorcycle and it needed a lot of muscling through corners. It was not so much that it was difficult to ride, but rather that it was a machine that needed to be ridden hard. One of its advantages was that, despite its size and power, it was beautifully balanced. The particular machine that Fogarty rode in 1992 (with chassis number 3FV000113) had previously been used by the Loctite racing team on short circuits in the 1991 season, being campaigned that year by Mark Philips and Terry Rymer. It was fitted with a special long kit swinging arm, Ohlins rear suspension unit and a factory bellcrank and linkages. The fuel tank was a special twenty-four-litre model, while the engine boasted a factory head, factory rods and crank, factory magnesium flat slide carburettors, kit dry clutch, 'C' kit gearbox, kit sump, Quill exhaust and factory ignition and wiring. Finally it sported a striking red and white livery, the racing colours of the Loctite Yamaha team.

So much for the machine, what about the rider? Neither of the two regular Loctite riders were available for the 1992 TT, so the team approached experienced racer Carl Fogarty to see if he would be interested. Born in Blackburn, Lancashire, Carl was the son of 1970s TT racer George Fogarty. Having grown up in a racing paddock it was natural for him to want to become a professional racer himself, and in the late 1980s Fogarty had been a factory Honda rider, appearing at the TT on numerous occasions alongside teammate Steve Hislop. He won three TT races in 1989 and 1990, before moving on to try his hand at MotoGP and World Superbikes. In the latter he had been using Ducati machinery, but he suffered constant reliability problems, which led to financial problems. In 1992 he was tempted by a big-money offer to return to the TT, riding for the Loctite Yamaha team. Fogarty remembered that although the OWO1 was not as fast as Honda's RVF or RC30, he had always wanted a chance to ride one, and held the model in great esteem. Former teammate Steve Hislop, meanwhile, was from Hawick, in the Scottish borders. Though he held the lap record on the Isle of Man he had likewise turned his back on the TT, only to be similarly tempted back to the Island in 1992 by an offer from Ron Haslam's Norton team. This package of rider and bike had been put together so hastily that there had been little time to organise any sponsorship. Thus the Norton went out in predominantly white livery, earning it the nickname 'White Charger'. Unfancied at first because of its unconventional rotary engine, the Norton proved to be exceedingly fast and Hislop threw down the gauntlet to Fogarty in the opening Formula 1 race, when he took second place. This was despite having to come in to remove the front mudguard in the pits, due to an overheating engine. Fogarty was in blistering form, and was leading that race by more than thirty seconds when his gearbox gave out at the Bungalow and he had to coast back down to the grandstand. The stage was now set for the Senior TT on the Friday, an epic duel between two of the titans of the 1980s and 1990s.

At the beginning of the race Fogarty was joint leader with Robert Dunlop, but the latter's challenge faded quickly, with a leaking oil seal contaminating his footrest and causing him to back off. From then on it was effectively a two-man battle between Hislop and Fogarty, but the Lancastrian soon lost the use of his rev counter, with the needle waving wildly. Soon after came brake problems, when the front pads were knocked back. There was a gap of only three seconds between the two rivals for most of the race when, on lap four, Hislop had a bad pit stop that cost valuable time. In the heat of the moment he had forgotten which was his bay, and force of habit had taken him towards his old stand from his earlier Honda days! There was more drama on the last lap when the exhaust on Fogarty's Yamaha began to disintegrate. Fogarty tells us about that momentous race:

> the lead changed after every lap and I was riding so hard that the bike was falling apart around me. None of the clocks were working, the front fork seal had gone, the rear brake arm was bent up, the rear shock was broken – the bike was an absolute mess. I was nine seconds behind at the start of the final lap, which was a lot to make up. To make matters worse, the exhaust blew coming over the mountain as I made that final push.

Carl Fogarty leans in at Quarterbridge in the 1992 Senior TT, aboard the 750cc Loctite Yamaha. (Bikesport Fottofinders archives)

After I had finished, I could hear the commentary over the tannoy, '....and here comes Hislop, he wins by four seconds...'[73]

In fact, Fogarty's exhaust started to disintegrate at Glen Helen, where the rear plate was picked up by one of the marshals as a souvenir, and he actually blew the wadding out of it going down the Cronk-y-Voddy straight. Photographs taken there at the time showed pieces of it littering the road. Fogarty continues:

To pull back five seconds was amazing and, in doing so, I had set a new lap record of 123.61mph... Okay, Steve had won the race, but I had always wanted to be the fastest man around the Isle of Man TT circuit. To me, on this occasion, that was better than race victory. 'Congratulations', I told Steve, 'but I've got the new lap record'. He obviously didn't believe me. 'I broke your lap record on the last lap,' I insisted. I could tell that he was a bit pissed off... I still maintain that no other rider on this planet could have matched what I did on that lap on that day. Not bad for my last ever lap around the circuit.[74]

It was said that directly after the race, Loctite team manager Rob McElnea was so embarrassed by the battered state of the bike that he quickly threw a tarpaulin over it and had it wheeled away to the paddock. After the 1992 TT it was put on display at the Loctite headquarters, until race-team owner Pete Beale purchased all of the Loctite team bikes at the end of the year. The other bikes were broken up for parts, but Beale kept the Fogarty machine intact. He used it himself only briefly, taking it to Daytona in 1993 where it was ridden by Mark Farmer (who gained a creditable eighth place with it, as the first non-factory bike to cross the finishing line). It also raced at the 1993 TT in the Formula 1 race. Today, after passing through the hands of several collectors and private owners, the Fogarty OWO1 is back on the Isle of Man, and forms part of the collections of Manx National Heritage. It is usually to be found on display in the Manx Museum in Douglas.

The 1992 Senior TT is still regarded by many as the greatest race in the long history of the event, surpassing even Mike Hailwood and Giacomo Agostini's famous battle in the 1967 Senior. Of the two competing

The 750cc Yamaha OWO1 as ridden by Fogarty in 1992 at the TT. (Courtesy of Manx National Heritage)

motorcycles, why choose the Yamaha as one of the top twenty-five all time great machines, ahead of Hislop's Norton? Hislop won the race, certainly, but to what degree was that due to his skill as a rider rather than the performance of the machine? To a great extent Norton's revival faded after 1992, but Hislop continued to score impressive wins and championship titles. In the end the Yamaha makes the cut firstly because it is a modern classic machine in its own right, and secondly for its astonishing performance on that day in 1992. Although Fogarty finished second, the bike set a lap record that stood for seven years, an incredible achievement. Not only that, but its association with the man who is arguably Britain's greatest living motorcycle racer makes it truly special. And if you disagree with this verdict, and feel that the Norton is the more significant machine, take heart. That motorcycle is also preserved, and can usually be seen at the National Motorcycle Museum in Birmingham.

Chapter 19

1000cc Honda SP1
(rider Joey Dunlop)
2000

The Honda SP1 ridden by Joey Dunlop at the 2000 TT was a special machine for a number of reasons. It took him to his first big bike win in twelve years, at the age of 48, when many people said it was no longer possible for him to achieve such a thing. The distinctive red motorcycle, which contrasted with his trademark yellow helmet, is also poignant in that it reminds his legions of fans of his final appearance at the event. Lastly, the details of its design and build are particularly interesting. The SP1 was a special, a 'bitsa' assembled in Britain from factory suspension, factory swinging arm and a more or less standard frame. However, it was the engine which was the jewel in the crown, requisitioned as it was from American Honda rider Aaron Slight's World Superbike machine, and looked after by his mechanic.

The rider, too, can only be described as special. Joey Dunlop was born in Ballymoney, Northern Ireland, in 1952. Growing up in the heartland of Irish road racing he naturally took an interest in setting up and competing on motorcycles, but for many years that was all it was – an interest or hobby – for his day job was as a publican. Even though he won his first TT in 1977, it was not for some years that he was signed up as a factory rider. He continued as a privateer, coming to the TT each year with his motley band of mechanics and supporters, and machines like the scruffy Rea Yamaha that somehow managed to steal wins from the 'established' teams. Ironically he was first signed by Suzuki in the early 1980s, before they inexplicably allowed Honda to poach him from under their noses. From then on, with consistent Honda works support, there was no stopping Joey.

Even though he was now a factory rider, Dunlop could never be described as a marketing man's dream. A man of few words and shy of publicity, he nevertheless managed to build up a legion of followers. His anti-hero status endeared him to thousands, even though he was no Barry Sheene (off the track at any rate). The best that Honda's marketing people managed to do was smarten him up a little, but it is fair to say that Joey was so valuable to the company that he could get away with pretty much what he liked.

The RC 51/VTR1000 used by Joey at the 2000 TT was Honda's latest weapon in the World Superbike wars, and was designated as an SP1 sub-model. The V-four Honda RC 45, while eventually making it to championship winner in 1997, was still considered inferior to Ducati's 916 and by the end of the final decade of the twentieth century it was ageing fast. Honda now decided to play Ducati at their own game. The original RC 51/VTR1000 was developed purely as a road bike, and has been thought of by many as a development of the earlier RC 45/VFR series, albeit with only two cylinders, although Honda did retain the V configuration of its predecessor. To be precise it was a 90-degree, 9-valve V-twin, and had fuel injection. Among a host of other innovative features, centrally mounted ram air-intake ducts routed cool pressurised air directly through the steering head structure into the ten-litre airbox, improving intake efficiency while slimming the aerodynamic profile. The ram airduct doubled as a front cowl stay, thereby also saving weight. Each cylinder head featured large 40mm intake and 34mm exhaust valves with a twenty-four degree valve angle. This provided a short, direct path for the air/fuel mixture entering the combustion chamber and resulted in increased power output. Gear-driven camshafts used three-axis drive gears to maintain accurate valve timing and durability at sustained high engine speeds. Specially developed head gaskets minimised distortion caused by head-bolt tightening, improving the seal and thereby maintaining combustion pressure for consistent high-power output. High-pressure programmed fuel injection delivered fuel at 50psi to two injectors per cylinder, mounted opposite each other in huge 54mm throttle bodies.

Among the achievements that this machine would notch up in its first year were the World Superbike championship, which it took in 2000 with Colin Edwards on board, while in endurance racing, a factory RC51 would win the most prestigious Japanese race of the year, the Suzuka Eight Hour event, in July of 2000 in the hands of 250cc Grand Prix rivals Tohru Ukawa and Daijiro Kato. Honda V-fours had been consistent winners in endurance racing, so Honda executives would doubtless be pleased that the new V-twin picked up where the company's previous bikes had left off. Before all this, however, came the drama of the Isle of Man TT.

Honda Britain had originally planned to contest the 2000 TT on Fireblades, but in the early part of the year upped their game to the newly introduced SP1. It was quickly arranged for Dunlop to ride one of Paul Bird's British Superbike spec SP1 machines at the event, but when he took it out at the North West 200 in early May he was comprehensively outpaced by the V&M Yamaha R1 of David Jefferies. Joey made it plain to Honda supremos that the firm would suffer a humiliating defeat on the Island at the hands of arch-rivals Yamaha if something was not done, and so a World Superbike quality engine was crated up and flown to the Isle of Man specially for his use.

The difference between this and a standard race kit engine was quite remarkable. Some claimed that it produced an additional 12bhp to deliver 175bhp. In simple terms this was because the race kit engine was built to different tolerances. It had to last a whole season's racing (about 3,000 miles) whereas it was accepted that the more finely tooled factory engine would have to be rebuilt after a mere 300 miles. The kit engine was also produced to a fixed cost, and had to be affordable by race teams on a budget (it sold for about £25,000), whereas with a full factory engine, cost was not an issue. In it, the cylinder heads and pistons raised the compression ratio to 13:1, using titanium conrods. Stronger valves and camshafts allowed the works motor to rev to 12,000rpm, about 1000rpm more than the kit engine. On the works engine both exhausts exited on the same side and then separated under the seat, which also necessitated the use of a non-standard, factory-built swinging arm that had to be flown in from Japan. This swinging arm had a special recess on the side to allow the exhaust pipes to travel along it, and the Honda mechanics in the UK had to fabricate special brackets to hold these in place, as none were available to them. The Dunlop bike also featured a quick-release system for the rear wheel, likewise borrowed from World Superbikes, which allowed for quicker pit stops. The remainder of Joey's hybrid SP1 mount comprised the frame and bodywork of James Toseland's British Superbike machine.

Some sources state that in fact two engines were shipped from Japan, and if this is the case, then it would appear that the only engine actually used at the TT was that of Aaron Slight, while the other, Colin Edwards's engine, was the spare. Photos of the bike on the Isle of Man show it in two colour schemes – the blue 'Vimto' colours of Paul Bird's racing team, and the Honda UK red and black. The Vimto bodywork was used during practice week, and replaced by Honda livery for the races.

It was David Jefferies who set the early pace in practice. Taking full advantage of the good weather, he recorded a lap at over 123mph on the Monday evening, only the third session of the week. He was clearly throwing down a gauntlet, but Joey Dunlop always rode at his own pace; over more than twenty years of racing on the Isle of Man he had never once cracked under pressure, and was not about to start now. His was a brand new bike, intended for the ultra-smooth short circuits of the World Superbike series, not the bumpy and uneven Mountain Course, and it would take some time to set up correctly. After the first lap of early morning practice the next day, Dunlop came straight back to the paddock to discuss any necessary changes with the assembled Honda technicians. While there was not much waving of arms or shouting, the body language said it all, and when Joey took his famous yellow Arai helmet off, his expression was one of granite. A few hushed words to the mechanics followed, some adjustments were made and then the booming V-twin was fired up and he was away for another lap. Joey looked more focussed and determined than many had ever seen him before, yet the handling problems he was experiencing just refused to go away. Finally, the night before the Formula 1 race, a set of 1999 vintage Dunlop tyres were flown to Honda race camp on the Island. They were fitted, and cured the machine's high-speed wobble instantly.

It is easy to embellish in retrospect, especially in view of events which followed, but many of those who were lucky enough to have seen the 2000 Formula 1 TT knew they had witnessed something particularly special, indeed the stuff of TT legend. It was unusual on the Isle of Man

Joey Dunlop aboard the SP1 flies over Ballaugh Bridge, 2000 Formula 1 TT. (Bikesport Fottofinders archives)

for the works Honda to be considered an underdog, but even Joey's own supporters doubted that at forty-eight years of age he still had the physical strength to wrestle with a superbike like this, and thought that his wins were now confined to the smaller classes. If Formula 1 day had dawned dry and bright, there could well have been an entirely different result. As it was, the conditions were damp and unpredictable, and thus would suit the Irishman well. This race, however, would not be about breaking lap records; that would be for later in the week. Under the watchful eye of Honda's first racing manager and now company president Mr Kawashima, Joey set off at a frantic pace. He was a man on a mission, and he knew the roads better than anyone in the mixed conditions. At Glen Helen, nine miles out, Joey was two seconds up on Michael Rutter, with his V&M Yamaha teammate David Jefferies another one second back in third. A major slide had dented Rutter's confidence on the opening lap and he had fallen back a further four seconds by Ramsey Hairpin, leaving Jefferies to take up the challenge. Joey, in contrast, was in his element. It was just like old times, and when he came into the pits to refuel at the end of lap two he was nine seconds up. Even stalling the bike in the stop box did not phase him, and he quickly restarted the motor.

Although the riders had already completed a full distance for a Grand Prix or Superbike race, there was still two-thirds of the race left, and Jefferies showed that he was not beaten yet. The Yamaha rider was now picking up speed to close the gap to four seconds going into the fourth lap. Sensing possible victory, Jefferies put in a huge effort to set the fastest lap of the race and edge ahead of Joey for the first time by a slender four seconds, but the speed of Dunlop's second pit stop put him back at the top of the leaderboard. For Jefferies, pace was now coming at the expense of reliability. The normally armour-plated V&M machine was starting to show the strain, and began to smoke badly. The clutch finally shattered at Ballig, and David Jefferies's race was over. With Rutter experiencing difficulties of his own due to a holed radiator, for the last 37¾ miles Dunlop was alone.

The fans cheered Joey all round that sixth and final lap, and there were emotional scenes as the bright red Honda came into the view of the packed grandstand. It was a moment few who saw it will ever forget. For Honda, it was a great day. Dunlop had repaid the faith they had shown in him. Not only was there pandemonium in the grandstands, where Joey was given a standing ovation, but the pit lane also roared itself hoarse. While he was being mobbed in the winner's enclosure, a reporter managed to get a few words from Joey: 'I never thought I'd win another Formula 1 race, but I've never had a bike this good... Its best bike I've ever ridden.'[75]

A smile from Joey Dunlop on the podium after the 2000 Formula 1 TT. (Bikesport Fottofinders archives)

At a private dinner that evening, Dunlop put his legendary shyness to one side to make the first speech that anyone who was there that night could ever remember him making. In spite of the fact that it was he who had just handed Honda an amazing victory, Joey wanted to thank Mr Kawashima for his help in getting him the bike. Less than one month later Dunlop, Honda's greatest star at the TT, was dead, killed in a crash at an obscure road race in Estonia, where he slid off the track and hit a tree.

There are curious parallels between the SP1 and Hailwood's RG500. Both were specially assembled from components of other world-class machines for a specific TT purpose, both were ridden by TT legends at the peak of their fame at the time, and both were used at their last appearance at the TT. The similarities don't end there – both riders were killed in tragic accidents not long after their historic rides. What does separate them, however, is that whereas the current whereabouts of the Hailwood RG500 is well known, that of Joey's machine is far more obscure. Certainly the machine that stood in the Manx Museum for some years afterwards was not the real thing: it was a realistic replica used by Honda in a parade lap, and supplied through the good offices of Bob McMillan, Honda UK boss at the time. Anyone who knew Joey well also knew that he could never even have sat on it. It is believed that four such replicas existed at one time, and they have certainly muddied the waters. In 2016 the Isle of Man Motor Museum at Jurby claimed to have on display the original SP1 from 2000, but to those in the know it was clearly the same replica that had previously been on show at the Manx Museum. It is certainly telling that the original machine – assuming it still exists – has not surfaced, given the continued interest in Joey Dunlop. Someone claiming to have had it 'authenticated' by Joey's mechanic offered what they said was the original SP1 for sale a couple of years after his death, but the truth of the matter is that Honda made no secret of the fact that the machine was disassembled by them directly after the 2000 TT. The engine would certainly have been needed for other events, and as a Honda insider pointed out at the time, politically it could not have remained in Britain. The US-based Honda World Superbike team had spent a million dollars developing their machines, and if the Honda hierarchy had given away the engine to a British BSB team, the fallout would have been toxic. Likewise the swinging arm, flown in from Japan, was needed back there for the Suzuka Eight Hour race, and was returned directly after the 2000 TT.

Be that as it may, the machine makes the cut for the top twenty-five TT machines, for delivering arguably Joey's greatest win, and certainly one of the most memorable. As a factory 'special' it also has a unique place in TT history, and stands as a testament to the ongoing importance Honda attaches to victory in the Isle of Man.

Chapter 20

Suzuki GSX R-1000 Superbike (rider David Jefferies) 2002

In the early 2000s a motorcycle appeared that set racetracks alight around the world. Like Suzuki's earlier RG500, their GSX R-1000 quickly became the 'must have' machine for aspiring racers on short circuits, in Grand Prix events and at the TT. It was highly effective, and yet it was affordable. In the hands of a rider from West Yorkshire named David Jefferies, it was a machine that would rewrite the record books on the Isle of Man, in the process winning both the Formula 1 and Senior TT in its first year on the Island. It is Jefferies's machine, in the colours of TAS Suzuki and campaigned at the 2002 Isle of Man meeting, which is the subject of our next chapter, and the twentieth in our series of top twenty-five TT machines.

David Jefferies was born in Shipley in 1972 and was the son of former TT rider Tony Jefferies. The family firm was a motorcycle dealership, and the Jefferies family perhaps have more claim than any other to being a TT 'dynasty'. At least four members of the family have competed at the event, over three generations. David began his TT career in 1996, and quickly established a reputation as one of the rising stars of the motorcycle racing world, with wins at the North West 200, Macau Grand Prix and other meetings. In 1999 and 2000 he raced in the red and yellow colours of V& M Yamaha, and he was the main challenger to Joey Dunlop at the 2000 TT. In both of these years he picked up a hat-trick of wins, enough to convince anyone who might still have had any doubt of his immense talent.

This was enough to bring him to the attention of Northern Ireland-based Temple Auto Salvage (TAS) Suzuki Racing. The team manager was Phillip Neill, but the outfit was owned by his father, Hector Neill. Hector's association with racing at the TT stretches back to the 1970s. He was a friend and sponsor of 1970s legend Tom Herron, and backed Norman Brown for his 1982 Senior TT-winning ride. There was no racing in 2001, due to foot and mouth disease restrictions, so the team's first appearance at the TT came in

2002. In the run-up to the meeting the TAS team made Jefferies a serious offer to join their set-up, and he appeared at that year's TT in the blue and white colours of TAS racing. At the time, Jefferies was one of the biggest names in British motorcycle racing and it was a coup for TAS to snatch him away from Jack Valentine's V&M team. However, as far as Jefferies was concerned it was was not just a case of money talking. He had seen close up what the TAS machinery was capable of, stating that: 'The Suzuki is the only bike that has passed me in a straight line while I've been riding the V&M Yamahas, so the bike's certainly quick enough.'[76]

He added on his website:

> I felt the opportunity of being with the TAS team was too good to miss... The Suzuki has been the all-powerful Superbike and the prospect of riding a 180bhp Superbike on the road circuits is going to be a real challenge.[77]

This time he was to be mounted for the big bike races aboard the newly released Suzuki GSX R-1000. It was powered by a 988cc four-cylinder liquid-cooled double-overhead cam engine with sixteen valves and fuel injection. Innovatively it used the same basic engine cases as Suzuki's 750cc model, plus the identical cylinder head. This allowed the firm's engineers to keep the bigger GSX-R's engine width the same, with just an incremental gain in height (14mm) and length (6mm). The motor was about eight pounds heavier (mostly due to a larger, stouter crankshaft), but weight loss in other areas of the chassis helped offset much of that gain. Employing the 750cc cylinder head meant the bore could be enlarged by only 1mm. Thus, in order to achieve the necessary displacement, the crankshaft stroke was increased by a whopping 13mm; this put the GSX-R in the same relatively undersquare bore/stroke league as the Yamaha R1, compared to the revvier, oversquare (bigger bore/shorter stroke) motors of the rival Honda CBR929RR and Kawasaki ZX-9R.

The Formula 1 and Senior TT-tuned engine could produce 183bhp, while even in Production category form it could still produce a blistering 159bhp, and in race trim this was complimented by an Akrapovic exhaust system, close-ratio gear cluster, carbon-fibre bodywork and Ohlins suspension. Since its emergence in 2001, the bike had proved itself to be a guided missile on race tracks around the world and there was now eager anticipation about what it could achieve on its TT debut, in the hands of popular 'DJ', as Jefferies was known. Ironically however, practically the only people who felt differently were Suzuki GB management. They were less convinced of success and, worried about potentially embarrassing publicity if their machines failed, had actually phoned Hector Neill and asked him not to put the name Suzuki on the side of the team transporter! Hector replied that it was too late, the wagon was already painted, and in any case there was nothing to worry about. Suffice it to say that by the end of race week, Suzuki could not have been more delighted that their name was in three foot high letters on the side of the van.

With the strongest engine in the 1000cc class, there could be no doubt that the 'gixxer' (as it was nicknamed) was a powerful bike, but Jefferies was more than capable of wrestling it under control and channelling the power in a useable way. However an indication of the effort involved in doing this comes from the fact that during practice week, Jefferies actually bent the retaining bolts for the footrests during every session, simply because he was putting so much force through them in order to get the bike to change direction on the bumpy section of the TT course after Ginger Hall. Overall, however, practice time was in short supply in 2002, as the first week was plagued by rain.

Things were better the following week, and as the rest of Britain began its commemoration of that year's Golden Jubilee, the Isle of Man had much of its own to celebrate; both glorious weather and TT racing had returned to the Island, after the enforced absence of the latter in the previous year with the foot and mouth crisis. The first race of the 2002 meeting was the Formula 1 TT, in which the Yorkshireman was the clear favourite (not least because of some blistering lap times set in practice). Unlike many other riders, Jefferies rarely got nervous before a race, nor did he have any of the superstitious rituals that many have (though he admitted that he would not go out as number thirteen!). However, just before the race began he was spotted walking towards the cemetery that lies behind the TT scoreboard. When asked about it later he said he had just gone over to say hello to a former TT rider buried there....

Right from the drop of the flag in that Formula 1 race Jefferies blew the opposition away, posting a lead of seven seconds by the first timing point at Glen Helen, nine miles out. He became the first man to circulate the course in under eighteen minutes, with a speed of 125.76mph on his first lap, and by the second he took the lap record to over 126mph, despite having to stop for fuel. This gave him a lead of a full minute over nearest rivals John McGuinness and Jim Moodie by the third lap. Disaster almost struck on the final circuit, however, when at Ramsey hairpin a gearbox problem almost cost him the race. Jefferies later told *Motor Cycle News*:

I nearly lost control of all bodily functions when I went for the next gear up only to hear the limiter cut in and nothing happen. I was really worried before I got third and just knew it was a gear selector fault that would only get worse if I tried to bang another gear in. I just left it alone and had to make do for the rest of the lap with only third. When I got to the Mountain Mile it was like the Mountain three miles because I was on the limiter all the way around. The most important thing for me was to concentrate on keeping the speed up because when it gets slow, you're not concentrating fully and that's when mistakes happen.[78]

The problem was caused by a small screw in the selector shaft working loose, and the team had known about the possibility of this problem since the previous week. Jefferies was also aware of it and so knew better than to try to change gear. Racing back over the mountain stuck in third gear was not without its challenges, however. He had no engine braking to slow him down going into corners, and got caught up in a tussle with a back marker into the bargain. Nevertheless, Jefferies finished first, with John McGuinness second and Ian Lougher third. To begin with the big Yorkshireman could not believe it, having been convinced that having ridden so hard he had thrown it all away on that last half lap, but the pit crew assured him that he had won. It was Suzuki's first victory in the Formula 1 race since Graeme Crosby's win in 1981, breaking Honda's almost twenty-year stranglehold on the event. Even so, Jefferies felt that the bike had even more potential and that he could have gone even faster on that last flying lap, were it not for the mechanical difficulties.

The next outing that week was the 1000cc Production TT. The three-lap race saw another dominant performance from David Jefferies, this time on a machine scarcely changed from one that could be bought in a shop, and on road-legal tyres. He took the win, breaking the race record in the process, from Suzuki teammate Ian Lougher in second with New Zealander Bruce Anstey in third position. It was now obvious that Jefferies was on a charge, and he claimed in an interview that as the week went on, he was only going to get faster. As his knowledge of the circuit grew, so did his confidence, and he now felt able to push flat out through some sections where, a year or so previously, he would have rolled off the throttle.

On the final day of race week, Senior Race day, road closures were delayed due to fog on the mountain section of the course, which prevented helicopter access. The first event of the day, the Production 600 TT, scheduled for a 10.45am start, finally got underway at 12 noon. By this time some fans had trickled away from the course to watch a crucial World Cup match between England and Argentina that kicked off at 12.30pm. However, the main event of the day, the Senior TT, finally got underway at 2.30pm. This race was to bring the curtain down on a week that had seen Jefferies utterly dominate the

David Jefferies lifts the Senior TT trophy for the final time, in 2002. (Bikesport Fottofinders archives)

big bike races. This time the race-prepared Suzuki ran perfectly; Jefferies was aided by the fact that his TAS teammate Ian Lougher overshot in the stop box at the top of the pit lane, and was penalised by five seconds (effectively torpedoing his chances of winning) and his main rival, John McGuinness on a Honda Fireblade, was left behind as he tried to catch him on the Sulby Straight. It is difficult to overstate just how significant Jefferies's win in the 2002 Senior was. On his second lap he set a new absolute lap record of 127.29mph, in the process shattering the Senior record as well. He also set a new race record of 124.74mph. He became the first man to win three TTs in a week in three consecutive years. His build and size, which in the early part of his career had counted against him, with many writing him off as too big to make a successful racer, had actually proved to be his secret weapon, for a course as bumpy and twisting as the TT, and a machine as powerful as the GSX-R, needed a great deal of upper body strength. Slightly built TAS teammate Ian Lougher admitted that it was exactly this that gave DJ his advantage: he had the strength in his arms to place the bike exactly where he wanted it. Jefferies summed up his feelings afterwards:

> The response from all the fans around the circuit was fantastic. The signals, the cheering – which you can actually hear at some of the popular spectator spots – and the programme-waving gives so much encouragement that it really eggs you on, which just helps the TT to be such a special event. And the star of the week? Well what else – the Suzuki GSX-R1000.[79]

It had been a truly astonishing week for TAS Suzuki, and Jefferies returned to the team for the TT in 2003, promising even greater achievements. Tragically he was killed in a crash during practice, when his machine skidded on oil. Every life lost is mourned, but Jefferies was all the more so by those who did not even know him personally, because he undoubtedly had more to give to the sport he loved, and had he lived would certainly have racked up more TT wins. After his death, the GSX-R from 2002, aboard which he had set such a blistering pace in the Senior, remained at TAS racing headquarters in a semi-disassembled state. It was only in 2010, when Suzuki celebrated the fiftieth anniversary of their arrival at the TT, and a special exhibition was staged at the Manx Museum, that the machine came out of mothballs, and was displayed in public for the first time in eight years. The bike remains part of the collection of historic machines owned by Hector and Philip Neill, and occasionally appears at other events. Unquestionably it finds a place among the pantheon of greatest-ever TT machines, as the machine which more than any other demonstrated the astonishing ability of its remarkable rider.

The 2002 Jefferies GSX -R1000 as it is today. (Author's collection)

Chapter 21

DMR 600cc sidecar outfit (riders Dave Molyneux/Dan Sayle/ Craig Hallam) 2003

Of the many sidecar outfits raced by the Isle of Man's Dave Molyneux over his thirty-year career, one in particular stands out above the others. It was aboard this machine that Molyneux achieved a goal which had eluded him for some six years – the breaking of the magical twenty-minute lap barrier in the sidecar TT. For a brief time this lightning-fast outfit was the hottest thing on three wheels, both on British short circuits and on the Isle of Man, before burning itself out in spectacular fashion. This is the story of that record-breaking machine, its rise to glory and its dramatic fall to earth.

Dave Molyneux is the most successful competitor on three wheels in the history of the Isle of Man TT. The son of a sidecar passenger, Molyneux took up racing literally as soon as he was able to do so, and in a neat illustration of the continuity of the event, he drew his inspiration from his boyhood hero, George O'Dell, whom he watched in action at the 1977 TT. Over the years 'Moly' as he is known to fans and pundits, has racked up an incredible tally of TT wins. Yet this is not the whole story, for early on in his racing career Molyneux decided to combine his skills from his day job as a mechanic and metal fabricator, with his knowledge of what really worked for him in a sidecar outfit.

Initially he faced some suspicion from parts suppliers, but gradually his reputation as a sidecar constructor grew, and today Dave Molyneux Racing (DMR) outfits are highly respected among the racing fraternity. Without recourse to blueprints or plans, and using a simple jig, he welds together tubular steel to create the frame to which the wheels, fuel tank, engine and eventually the bodywork of a racing sidecar outfit will be attached. Through many years of trial and error he has worked out the optimum positions for these components, in order to make the machine handle and corner in the most effective way. In the winter of 2003–04 in his unassuming workshop at Regaby outside Ramsey, he began work on a new machine which would both shake the world of sidecar racing at the TT, and have dramatic personal consequences for Molyneux himself.

Since 1998, Molyneux had enjoyed factory support from Honda Britain, and in the spring of 2004 the firm supplied him with a new powerplant – a 600cc fuel-injected engine, of the type found on the firm's CBR600 series, and it was in order to accommodate this engine that the new machine was built. Sidecar races at the TT were now run under Formula 2 regulations, which allowed for four-cylinder four-stroke engines. Previous fuel-injected engines from Honda had not worked well in a sidecar outfit, but now a lot of early difficulties had been resolved, and the new engine promised to have awesome amounts of power. With support from local sponsor Martin Bullock, and Sulby man Dan Sayle as passenger, the combination of men and machine proved its potential at the 2004 TT. They were fastest in every practice session and took victory in both sidecar races with ease.

In Race A the Manx duo took control from the start line, and remained so throughout the three-lap outing. On the second circuit they reached 112.61mph, to come within an ace of the lap record (set by Molyneux in 1999). Even a rattle that developed within the engine and forced them to slow on the last lap did not prevent them from winning by fifty-nine seconds, a truly commanding margin. In the second sidecar race of the meeting, Molyneux achieved his third TT double in eleven years. This time he and Sayle went even faster, breaking the 1999 lap record with a best speed of 113.17mph on lap two. Only a badly blistered rear tyre forced them to relax the pace a little on lap three, Molyneux later telling *Motor Cycle News*: 'We had a couple of major slides so I knew the back tyre was going off.'[80]

The final 'touring' lap allowed second-placed driver Nick Crowe to take almost twenty seconds out of their lead, but it was still another resounding victory for Molyneux and Sayle. Having won in a race time of one hour, one minute and 4.2 seconds, the magical sub-twenty-minute lap, a personal target he had set himself back in 1999, seemed now to be almost within Molyneux's reach. However, despite all this early success with the new machine, 2005 opened with some difficulties. Practice week was beset with mechanical problems, particularly with the engine management system. By the end of the week Molyneux, again with Dan Sayle in the chair, had not even qualified. He had done two untimed laps only in the first Saturday practice session, with constant breakdowns meaning that by the Friday he had yet to complete a timed lap. Molyneux later remembered:

By the Friday night the pressure was really on, but we went out and did two laps under twenty minutes, the first time that had ever been done. I'd had a lot of earache during the week, people saying the pressure was on, and if we didn't qualify then we wouldn't be able to race, blah blah blah. I just thought, 'Oh, give us a break.' We'd been out on the Saturday night, and did two laps with the bike straight out of the crate. We knew what speed we had done that night and so did they, but we'd still been getting these jibes thrown at us all week that we wouldn't be on the grid if we didn't get a lap of practice in that Friday night. Well we got those laps in, and I think it was Chris Kinley, the radio commentator, who came up to us afterwards and said, 'Dave, you've made history, the first ever sub-twenty-minute laps.' I was pretty cool about it and just said, 'Oh well, at least we've qualified!'[81]

The first sidecar race of the 2005 TT was a less than auspicious occasion, with poor weather contributing to the difficulties experienced by the crews. The road was damp, and at times during the race it was actually raining. Nevertheless, Molyneux set a blistering pace right from the flag, putting in a first lap at nearly 110 miles per hour, from a standing start in wet conditions. In the long run, however, the Regaby man was to fall victim to the same technical problems that had dogged him during practice. A plug cap coil had burned out, and the engine began to misfire on one cylinder. The Manx duo pulled in and retired, at a point in the race in which they held a forty-five second lead, one of the biggest in Molyneux's career. It was a disappointing result to say the least, but the sheer speed of the outfit was clear to see.

Between races, Molyneux was able to identify and finally fix the technical gremlin that had caused so many problems, and in a final lap of practice before Sidecar Race B the potential of the machine showed itself quite clearly, with a time once again under twenty minutes. The 2005 Sidecar B race was an electrifying affair, with Molyneux and Sayle putting in three laps under twenty minutes, with the first-ever sidecar race average under an hour and setting a 116mph lap record into the bargain. This amazing feat was achieved in spite of the fact that on the final lap (and almost within sight of the grandstand) a wheel bearing had collapsed, meaning that the machine had to be coasted in and across the line to take its third TT win.

From its first arrival in 2004 the Honda fuel-injected 600cc unit had the potential to be explosive, but in combination with the chassis that Molyneux had built to house it, and with the refinements and developments he had made over the course of two years, everything had come together into an outstanding package. He had no reason to think that 2006 would not bring further refinements and even greater power and speed, and the early part of that year certainly gave every indication that this would be the case. Now with former passenger Craig Hallam back aboard, the pairing began the season by contesting short circuit meetings in England. Molyneux recalls:

> We won the first two rounds of the British [Formula 2 Sidecar] Championship by a street mile, and when we went into the TT that year we were leading the Championship. It's really not an exaggeration to say that at that particular point in time we were in a different league from everyone else. Wet or dry conditions, it made no difference; there were guys there who professed to be wet-weather specialists, but we just blasted past them, in fact Craig said to me at one point, 'This is ridiculous, it's too easy Dave.' So we went into the TT in a strong position...[82]

With engine refinements and tuning by Dave Hagen of Evomoto, the DMR 600cc outfit again promised fireworks. The two engines supplied by Honda used standard parts, but Hagen's modifications were designed to wring extra ounces of power from them. One such change involved modifying the crankcases, by making holes so that the bottom end breathed better as the pistons rose and fell. Baffles were also fitted in the sumps to reduce oil starvation. Unlike the engine of a solo outfit, which leans into a bend, in a sidecar engine centrifugal force on a corner tends to drive the oil to one end of the sump and away from where it is needed. It is well known that fitting baffles in the sump can reduce this effect, and the consequent engine wear and tear. Other modifications remain closely guarded secrets in the competitive world of the race engine tuner.

Sure enough, the Molyneux outfit continued to rip up the record book at the 2006 TT. On the Wednesday evening of practice week, it set a new lap record from a stationary position; the achievement was all the more incredible because a standing start would normally mean giving away anything between ten and fifteen seconds on a flying lap, but the machine completed the circuit some two seconds faster than Molyneux's previous best time. The lap was timed officially at 19 minutes 28 seconds, amazingly fast. It seemed at that time that nothing could match this outfit, or indeed prevent it from easily claiming another two TT wins. The following evening the duo went out again, not with the intention of breaking any lap records, but merely to make sure they had given themselves the maximum possible amount of familiarisation time before race week. Molyneux recalls that night:

> So we set off with with all new tyres and chain and brake pads, and by the time you get to Ballacraine all that stuff is bedded in, its well and truly

Dave Molyneux and Craig Hallam power the DMR 600cc sidecar outfit through a corner during practice for the 2006 TT. (Author's collection)

bedded in, and so you can light the thing up a bit, start to go a lot quicker if you feel comfortable, and I'd never felt more comfortable in twenty years of racing round the TT mountain circuit than I did that night. I don't have a great recollection of what happened next that evening, or an understanding of why it happened.[83]

As the machine approached Rhencullen, between the fifteenth and sixteenth milestones beyond Kirk Michael village, all seemed normal. Molyneux took a tight line on the right-hander at the top of the hill, which was extremely bumpy, but which gave a good line going into the next bend, a left-hander. However, as the bike approached the jump it became unstable, running on the edge of the front tyre and making it hard to control. At 140mph, as it went over the jump, the outfit flipped. Trapped underneath, Molyneux skidded down the road, fighting with the machine to free himself as he did so. As it hit a stone wall, he parted company with it and staggered to his feet. In the minutes that followed, he stared back up the hill in disbelief, unable to comprehend what had just happened. When the bike eventually stopped sliding and dug in, it went end over end, righted itself and came to rest back on its wheels. In the dramatic events beforehand, however, it had been doused in high octane race fuel; as it had travelled down the road, the top of the airbox had worn away, exposing the fuel rail, which had also come into contact with the road. The friction caused sparks that set the outfit instantly alight. With two laps' worth of race fuel still on board and highly flammable carbon fibre bodywork, it went up like a roman candle. After getting quickly out of the road for fear of being hit by the following outfit, Molyneux took stock of his own injuries, which were severe:

> I walked into a nearby garden, and a kind gentleman from the house came out to see if I was OK. I was holding my right arm [which] was four inches longer than it should have been, and it didn't feel as if it was connected somehow. I knew as well that I'd taken a heavy smash in the right shoulder, because it wasn't there, it was now inside my ribcage. The guy from the house looked as scared as anyone I've ever seen, poor guy, he'd seen the whole thing happen. The marshals must have been shocked at the incident as well, but they reacted amazingly. I take my hat off to the marshals because its a hell of a job they've got to do, and the concern on their faces after just witnessing a 140 mile an hour crash, and then the machine going on fire, was obvious. I heard one guy shouting, 'Where is he?' They must have thought I'd been fired over a hedge or something, but then they saw me in the garden. I could see the bike was burning fiercely now but I was resigned to the fact that there was nothing I could do about it.[84]

After many months of medical treatment, including an operation to correct damage to his dislocated shoulder, Molyneux returned to the TT in 2007. Again it was on a self-built outfit, with a Honda engine on board. Although it was more or less identical to the bike he had lost in the previous year's crash, he was unable to replicate its characteristics. This, coupled with the lack of time available to develop the engine, makes Molyneux's double win aboard that outfit in 2007 all the more remarkable. As for the burned out 2003 machine, which had achieved so much in such a short space of time, it went on to become part of the collections of Manx National Heritage. Looking beyond the obviously charred and blackened metalwork and fabric, evidence of the severity of the impact at Rhencullen that night is clearly apparent.

The date is 28 June 2006, and Dave Molyneux surveys the burned-out wreckage of his machine in his workshop on the Isle of Man, following the horrific crash four weeks previously. (Author's collection)

The front brake disc is bent, and the fuel rail shows unmistakable scuff marks from contact with the road. It is, however, a testament to its builder's skill that the machine survived the impact largely intact, without breaking up. It is incredible to think that given Molyneux's achievements in the sidecar TT over his thirty-year career, there are other outfits from his own stable that might vie for a position in the top twenty-five TT machines. However, it is this 2003 machine, winner of three races on the Isle of Man and breaker of the twenty-minute-lap barrier, which makes the cut. A true TT titan.

Chapter 22

Superstock Suzuki GSX R-1000 (rider Bruce Anstey) 2007

New Zealand's Bruce Anstey has been one of the most consistent performers at the TT since his debut at the event in 1996, and for a number of years until the arrival of Michael Dunlop he was arguably the main threat to the dominance of John McGuinness. Our next TT Titan, his Suzuki GSX R-1000 from 2007, makes the cut because the motorcycle represents one of Bruce's finest moments at the TT, in the class in which he feels most comfortable and with which he is most closely associated: the Superstock race. It also represents an era in which Suzuki dominated this event – it was Anstey's fourth Superstock TT win on the trot, an unprecedented achievement in itself, and Suzuki's sixth. Finally, in terms of pure aesthetics it represents one of the classiest guises which Suzuki or any other manufacturer has ever appeared in at the TT – the sleek black and silver of Relentless by TAS racing.

The 2007 TT generally was memorable for many reasons. The fact that it was the centenary of the event only added to the usual carnival atmosphere. There were parade laps, re-enactments of the first TT race at St John's, and former riders returned, in some cases after years away. Many thousands of extra visitors flocked to the Island, and were treated to the sight of some thrilling racing. Northern Ireland's TAS Suzuki team took spectators' breath away when they appeared at the meeting for the first time in the stylish black livery of their new headline sponsor, the Relentless energy drink (produced by the Coca-Cola company). It was part of the brand's promotional strategy to associate themselves through sponsorship with extreme sports, and they competed at this and subsequent TT races as 'Relentless Suzuki by TAS.' They made such an impression on fans that a black Relentless T-shirt was the 'must-have' item of the fortnight, and stocks soon ran out. Under the name TAS Suzuki, the team (which was run by Northern Ireland-based father and son Hector and Philip Neill), had competed at the TT since 2002. Relentless Suzuki went into the 2007 TT with two riders, long-term associate of the team

Bruce Anstey's breathtaking 2007 Superstock-winning Suzuki. (Courtesy of Manx National Heritage)

Adrian Archibald (also from Northern Ireland), and Bruce Anstey, who had ridden for them in the form of TAS Suzuki since 2004.

New Zealander Bruce Anstey was born at Wellington in 1969, but has Manx ancestry on his mother's side. He was inspired to begin racing after a family holiday to the Isle of Man in 1978, when he watched Mike Hailwood win in his TT comeback. Anstey has only ever really wanted to compete on road courses, and made his competitive debut at the famous Wanganui Cemetery Circuit in his native New Zealand in 1990. He made his first appearance at the TT in 1996, remembering that back then there was none of the preparation and advice available to newcomers to the TT today. Anstey recalls that at his first practice session he was just given an orange hi-viz bib, and told 'off you go'. Having survived two brushes with cancer in the meantime, he took his maiden victory in the 2002 Lightweight race. Since then he has proved himself to be one of the most consistent riders at the event, notching up regular wins and places in the top three. Anstey's reputation for dependability and familiarity with the podium was further enhanced by the fact that in 2006 he had set (unofficially) the fastest speed ever recorded at the TT up to that point, 206mph at the end of the Sulby Straight. His easy-going and laid-back manner have made him a firm favourite with fans, his nickname 'Smiler' saying a lot about his personality, and it is often said that if he gets out of bed on the right side on the morning of a race, he is virtually unbeatable. The more immediate challenge is sometimes to get him out of bed in the first place, because whereas some riders get little sleep the night before a race, Anstey famously often slumbers until the mechanics or pit crew knock on the door of his caravan! For relaxation, he is sometimes to be found in the paddock area behind the TT grandstand practising his favourite hobby of tinkering with radio-controlled cars and helicopters. Relentless team boss Phillip Neill, speaking of him in 2007, recognised that Anstey is a true individual, and, when he was delivering the goods for the team on the track, it was very much a hands-off approach from the team principals:

> He's a difficult character to get to know and needs to be managed in a totally different way to any other rider I've known. I've learned that in the five years he's ridden for us, but I know there's a particular way to get the best out of him and I don't ever pressure him.[85]

Speculation was rife among Suzuki fans in 2007 that the firm's newest model would rip up the track at the TT. Nicknamed the Gixxer, the motorbike had been incredibly successful around the world up to that point, and consequently had a cult following. The Suzuki had been a leader on the track for several years, with its excellent chassis, brakes and super-strong motor, but the new-for-2007 version was even better. Comparing the power and torque curves of the new and previous generation Gixxers revealed that the 2007 design featured more over-rev than the 2006 model, and as a result did sacrifice some low-end power for its broader spread of muscle, although peak horsepower output had been increased considerably. This change in philosophy was intended to get the bike around the track quicker, by making it easier for the rider to go fast consistently. Compared to the Honda CBR and Kawasaki ZX, the GSX-R was lacking some punch below 9,000rpm, but there was a method to Suzuki's madness in this area.

The Gixxer power curve mimicked that of the Yamaha R1, in that the Suzuki also had a dip through the 6,000–8,000 range (although it did not feel as mundane as the Yamaha because, although it tapered off a little through the middle of the range, it came back on like a hurricane when the tach needle swept past the 9,000 position). On the track the Suzuki was still as much of a smooth-running, fire-breathing monster as there ever was. It still boasted a superb combination of manageable power delivery, light steering and nimble chassis, to ensure that it could handle any type of track it encountered.

Despite tipping the scales at a portly 436lb, the heaviest of its equivalent group of machines, and fourteen pounds over the lightweight CBR, it still managed to hold the weight well, and maintained a level of balance that encouraged its rider to tip it in harder and faster lap after lap. Writing about it in *Motorcycle Daily*, journalist Vitor Martins commented:

> There is no teasing this animal; this ultra-new GSX R-1000 has the same power as the most potent superbikes from about 5 years ago... Suzuki has usually offered the most powerful superbikes, and this year when all of them are rolling with 180 horsepower the GSX-R should, by tradition, go a bit farther... We asked ourselves how far the manufacturers will go with horsepower increases... But Suzuki is Suzuki, and it has a tradition of introducing the most powerful superbike of the moment. And it does not fall short when they say that their new beast offers not less than 185 horsepower... The chassis of the 2007 GSX R-1000 is more compact and light than the previous model (although overall weight is up slightly), the swingarm is stronger and the fork has been improved by a highly elaborate anti-friction treatment, as well as both high and low speed compression damping adjustments. The new brakes feature 310mm discs clamped by four piston, radial mounted calipers, powered by a radial master cylinder... The truth is that this new superbike feels much lighter, changes direction far easier and initiates turn-in more quickly than its predecessor, but we noticed that it drifted wide on corner exits; nonetheless, this improved when we increased fork compression damping... The 2007 GSX R-1000 is charged with the responsibility of retaking the superbike crown for Suzuki, both on the street and on the track. In our opinion... this very powerful, but amicable sport bike has everything it needs to compete for the top spot, both on the track and on the street this year.[86]

Anstey gave the fans a taster of what they might expect during practice week, when he posted the fastest lap in the Superstock class with this machine. However, it was not an auspicious start to race week at the 2007 meeting when he was forced to retire in the opening event, the Superbike TT. It was to be a different story on the Tuesday, when the Relentless team wheeled out the Superstock spec GSX R-1000 at the beginning of the four-lap race for showroom machinery. The only concession to the racetrack aboard this otherwise standard road bike was the rear tyre, made from a special compound from Pirelli that would withstand the gruelling race without needing to be changed.

Anstey, who has something of a reputation as a slow starter who needs time to get into his stride in a race, must have got out of bed on the right side on this particular morning. He set a blistering pace right from the flag, smashing the lap record with an astonishing 128.29mph first lap from a standing start, shattering teammate Archibald's record from 2005 (also set on a Suzuki). In lap two he went even faster, at 128.34mph, putting him over twenty seconds ahead of main challenger John McGuinness. He even bettered the latter's best lap from the Superbike race earlier in the week (though improved weather conditions between the two races also contributed). His final two laps were almost as fast, even though he pitted for fuel on lap three. Anstey was powering ahead and he added to his lead between each and every checkpoint, also leading the race on the road. None of the Honda riders, even the official HM Plant pairing of McGuinness and Ian Hutchinson, could come anywhere close to catching him, and Anstey won the Pokerstars-sponsored event by over forty seconds, an astonishing margin.

The reserved New Zealander later revealed that he was actually more worried by the threat posed by Irishman Martin Finnegan aboard his MV Agusta R312, after he had come in third-fastest in practice. Anstey told the press afterwards:

I knew I needed a good first lap and was worried about Finnegan. I wanted to push as hard as I could to get clear of him. Then I caught John [McGuinness] on the second lap and once I got by him I got my head down. The bike was handling superbly. I grew up racing production bikes and they seem to suit me.[87]

He also added:

The bike was going really well. I was quite nervous but it went really well for me. That last lap it was quite weird because I got held up quite a bit (by later starters).[88]

The last word on this memorable victory really belongs not to the quietly spoken and modest New Zealander, but to second-placed man John McGuinness. At the post-race press conference, McGuinness was bemused by Anstey's blistering pace, which left him and other contenders standing, and summed up the race succinctly saying 'Bruce really pulled our pants down out there today'. Suzuki continued to assert its dominance over the Superstock event with a win by Australian Cameron Donald, also in Relentless colours, in 2008. To celebrate the team's remarkable success, a limited edition black

Anstey roars off the Mountain and takes the turn at Creg-ny-Baa, 2007 Superstock TT. (Courtesy of TT Press Office)

A beaming Bruce Anstey after the 2007 Superstock victory, his fourth consecutive win in this class. (Courtesy of TT Press Office)

and silver replica, styled after Donald and Anstey's machines, was released by the company that year.

After the 2007 TT, Anstey was able to acquire the Superstock-winning machine from the Relentless team, and it now forms part of his personal collection. It has occasionally been seen on display, most notably in the 2010 Suzuki anniversary exhibition held at the Manx Museum in Douglas. The 2007 Superstock Suzuki makes the top twenty-five machines by virtue of the fact that it is an iconic machine in its own right. Add to this mix the association with Anstey (a figure who will surely go down in history as a TT great), the 2007 Centenary TT, and the stylish Relentless livery, and you have an undoubtedly potent combination.

Chapter 23

1000cc Honda
(rider John McGuinness)
2009

Morecambe's John McGuinness quickly established himself as the man to beat at the TT in the early part of the twenty-first century. Growing up, his boyhood hero was Joey Dunlop and his driving ambition was to emulate Dunlop's achievements at the TT. As a teenager McGuinness collected cockles on Morecambe beach in order to pay for a race bike, and at his first appearance at the event in 1996 he was voted best newcomer, an early indication of his talent. In his early years at the TT McGuinness competed on a wide variety of machinery. He briefly rode Ducatis and was also part of the AIM Yamaha team, before becoming part of the official Honda UK factory team in 2006. Since then, McGuinness has remained the only rider consistently in that team, though numerous teammates have passed through the ranks and ridden alongside him, notably Ian Hutchinson, Conor Cummins and Steve Plater. Although McGuinness has ridden a number of machines in his Honda years, one in particular stands out for the sheer consistency of its performance, and has earned a place in this collection of top twenty-five TT machines.

That motorcycle is part of the Honda Fireblade dynasty, specifically a CBR1000RR. The machine was part of a series that had undergone more or less continuous development since the 1990s, though the Fireblade model as we know it now dates from 2004. It was the type on which McGuinness took Senior TT victories in both 2006 and 2007, and has a 999cc liquid-cooled inline four-cylinder engine with fuel injection. With the 2008 redesign the engine was given a completely new cylinder block, head configuration and crankcase with lighter pistons, though the most obvious outwardly visible changes from the earlier Fireblade design were two scoops located in the front of the fairing, feeding ram air into an enlarged air box, and a revised exhaust system, which was no longer a centre-up underseat configuration. The new exhaust was a side-slung design in order to increase mass centralisation and compactness while mimicking a Moto GP-style. By 2009 the model was in its tenth generation, and with a major anniversary for Honda in that year (the fiftieth anniversary of its arrival at the TT), it was decided to build a new and improved machine specifically for McGuinness (in itself an indication of his seniority in the team), which incorporated elements of Honda's long experience in World Superbike racing, and also specific aspects to tailor the motorcycle for conditions at the Isle of Man TT.

Development began at Honda Racing UK's headquarters in Louth, under the direction of race-team manager Neil Tuxworth. The brakes were supplied by Brembo and were of World Superbike specification, while the chassis, in contrast, was specially developed for the TT, with full factory Showa suspension. The engine was capable of 14,500rpm, producing 210bhp and giving a top speed of 200mph, and included race kit components such as pistons and cams, supplied by Honda Racing Corporation (HRC). HRC is a separate arm of the Honda company, entirely independent and with its own budgets and management. Its purpose is to develop new racing engines and technology and supply it to Honda-supported teams around the world. Japanese firm Showa, meanwhile, are one of the world's largest producers of shock absorbers for the automotive industry. Showa suspension staff were

The 2009 1000cc Honda Fireblade built for John McGuinness. (Courtesy of Manx National Heritage)

on hand at a special pre-TT testing session at Castle Combe racing circuit in Wiltshire to assist with setting up the suspension in accordance with McGuinness's wishes.

With Honda Racing in a three-year sponsorship deal with Newcastle-based Hitachi construction equipment importers HM Plant, the bike made its first appearance at the 2009 TT in the distinctive orange and black livery of that company. In the first event of the 2009 meeting, the Dainese Superbike TT, the machine took a convincing victory and McGuinness scored his fifteenth Isle of Man win. The HM Plant Honda rider took the victory effectively unchallenged, leading all six laps and setting a new record with a 130.422mph lap during his second turn of the circuit. In the rain-delayed Senior at the end of the week, McGuinness again set a blistering pace aboard the machine, breaking his own lap record and setting a new fastest speed of 131.578mph. The race ended prematurely for McGuinness when his chain broke on lap four, handing victory to teammate Steve Plater.

It was a different story the following year, when the Honda team were dogged by problems all through race week, and an electrical fault caused McGuinness to pull up in both the Superbike and Senior races. These issues were resolved by the time of the next TT, and 2011 was to prove a much more auspicious year. In the Dainese Superbike race on Saturday, under clear skies and in optimal conditions, John McGuinness (now riding under the Honda TT Legends banner) used the machine to grab the sixteenth TT victory of his career, overcoming an early challenge from Bruce Anstey to put his name at the top of the leaderboard. On lap one McGuinness was leading Gary Johnson by just over a second, with Anstey running steady back in third. As usual McGuinness was putting in a quick first lap, but the Kiwi rider was matching his pace and by the end of the first lap both competitors were lapping at over 130mph. Just over halfway through McGuinness was in control, with more than a twenty-second lead ahead of Guy Martin, as Johnson was issued a thirty-second penalty for breaking the pit lane speed limit. The final lap was a breeze for McGuinness, as he coasted across the line for the win.

The 2011 Isle of Man TT ended on a high for the Morecambe rider with a sensational Senior race that saw him storm to his seventeenth victory. The riders had a tense wait for the race to begin, as rainfall in certain areas of the 37¾-mile course led officials to postpone the start three times. It eventually went ahead at 5.15pm under a clear blue sky with near-perfect conditions. McGuinness started the race in the number one slot and by the end of lap two he was running in third position behind Guy Martin and Bruce Anstey. A characteristically slick pit stop from the Honda TT Legends crew enabled him to make up valuable time and by the Ramsey Hairpin on lap three he

McGuinness aboard the HM Plant-liveried Honda in the 2009 Senior TT. (Courtesy of TT Press Office)

had stolen the lead from Martin. McGuinness controlled the rest of the race in spectacular style, widening the gap sector-by-sector and lap-by-lap to keep his rivals at bay and claim the deserved top spot. Neil Tuxworth, the team manager later commented:

> We came here to do two races and we won them both so it's been fantastic, a 100% success for the team. John has done a fabulous job... As always, the team in the pits has done brilliantly, pulling back time to enable John to take the lead. The bike has gone superbly and we've had no problems at all. We're over the moon![89]

McGuinness added his own perspective on events:

> I can't remember being pushed that hard in a superbike race for a very long time. It took me a lap or so to get into the rhythm of the superbike

again and I made the odd little mistake at the beginning there. I settled down after lap two, we had a mega pit stop and after that I was just going for it. On laps three and four I was pushing really, really hard and after another good pit stop I was able to run round on the last two laps with enough pace to stop Guy catching me. He made me work for it though! I want to thank the whole team and everyone who is behind the scenes making this happen – without them I wouldn't be in the position I'm in now. I'm so proud of winning my 17th win.[90]

Again the Dainese Superbike race kicked off events at the 2012 Isle of Man TT. In this race McGuinness was aided by two very quick and efficient pit stops by his crew. The first pit stop came after the second lap, after McGuinness set a race-best speed of 130.382mph on the Mountain Course. McGuinness held a 2.16-second lead over Wilson Craig Honda's Cameron Donald when they both entered the pits, but McGuinness emerged with a six-second lead. Donald reduced that lead to 3.8 seconds during the third lap, but couldn't maintain the pace, and McGuinness regained a 6.2-second lead at the end of lap three. McGuinness continued to separate himself from the other riders and after a pit stop on lap four, his margin grew to thirteen seconds. McGuinness pushed his lead to about eighteen seconds before easing up on the final lap to finish in a time of 1:46:03.06, translating to an average speed of 128.078mph. However, there was no opportunity to add to the tally, as in an unprecedented move the 2012 Senior TT was cancelled due to bad weather.

2013 brought about a change in events as McGuinness finished only third in the Superbike race, even though he managed to post a new lap record of 131.671mph. Normal service was resumed in the Senior TT. The Senior race was delayed after a red-flag incident, which involved a rider crash and injuries to spectators. Once the course was cleared of emergency personnel and the race was restarted, it appeared that new sensation Michael Dunlop was set for yet another TT victory. However, McGuinness broke into the front position on the second circuit of the Mountain Course, turning in a 131.272mph lap in the process. Dunlop continued to follow McGuinness on the timing throughout, but lost time at both pit stops. On the final lap McGuinness maintained his advantage en route to TT win number twenty. In a Honda TT Legends press release, McGuinness stated:

It feels absolutely fantastic to win today and if there's one race to win, it's the Senior... I've had a good week but a win's escaped me so do it today with the sun shining and thousands of fans waving me all the way is brilliant. The conditions were incredible, the bike was fantastic and with two superb pit stops we got the job done. I still feel really sharp and I hit all my apexes on the final lap so with a Honda 1-2-3, the job's a dream![91]

It was an amazing end to an amazing career for the McGuinness CBR1000RR, which was retired after the 2013 meeting. It had delivered five TT wins in five years for McGuinness, and helped Honda to maintain a dominant position at the TT as the event entered its eleventh decade. At the time of writing the machine, in its 2009 HM Plant livery, is on display at the Manx Museum in Douglas. Honda technicians were careful to preserve the bodywork with the flies from the Superbike win still on it, and damage to the windscreen caused by a bird strike. It makes the top twenty-five by virtue of its sheer consistency – few other machines can claim to have delivered such a panoply of big bike wins and lap records – and its association with a rider who has stamped his authority on the TT in the first decade of the twenty-first century, and in doing so became the 'man to beat' at the event.

Chapter 24

Padgett's 1000cc Honda (rider Ian Hutchinson) 2010

In recent years Ian Hutchinson (the so-called Bingley Bullet, or 'Hutchy' to his fans) has blazed a trail through TT record books. It is a testament to Hutchinson's strength of character that he not only defied his doctors, who wanted to amputate his damaged leg following a serious accident in 2011, but has also fought his way back into racing form. Even more than this, he has exceeded his own performances prior to that incident to take podium positions and race wins in such consistent fashion that he has been practically in a league of his own in recent years. But it is to 2010, before that accident, that we must return in order to find the next in our series of top twenty-five TT machines.

Hutchinson (who had previously raced at the Isle of Man TT in the colours of the official HM Plant Honda factory team, and already had three TT wins under his belt) had signed once again for local West Yorkshire team Padgetts in 2010. One of the largest of the independent competitors, the family-run Padgetts team are based at the Batley motorcycle dealership of the same name, and have a long history of competition at the TT. Manager Clive Padgett is one of the best-known and most-respected figures in the TT paddock, having a lifetime of experience in setting up and racing motorbikes (it was Clive who sold a young John McGuinness his first racing motorcycle). Despite this experience, it was still something of a David and Goliath encounter between the family-run team and the might of the Honda UK Racing operation, which had full HRC support and all the expertise that the Japanese firm could supply. This is what made the 2010 TT such a remarkable and memorable event, for Hutchinson and Padgetts not only bettered the official Honda entry, but Hutchinson also won all five of the solo events for conventional (not electric) motorbikes, the only time in the long history of the TT that this has ever happened.

Padgetts took three motorbikes to the 2010 TT, two CBR 1000RR Fireblades (one each in Superbike and Superstock trim) and a CBR 600 RR. It is the second of these three which, with some justification, takes position number twenty-four in the top twenty-five TT machines of all time. Some might argue that any of those three race-winning machines could make the list, but Hutchinson himself counts the Superstock bike as the best of the bunch. The others were new machines in 2010, but the 'Stocker' already had race-winning form from 2009, being the machine that took victory in both the 2009 Royal London 360 Superstock race at the TT, and the Ulster Grand Prix of that year. It would go on to win the 2010 Superstock TT, 2010 UGP and a British Superstock championship race, setting two TT lap records along the way.

The 2009 Royal London 360 Superstock TT was a battle royale in its own right, and deserves closer comment. Hutchinson eventually took victory, defeating Guy Martin by 8.77 seconds in the process. It was a thrilling contest, and for the majority of the race the lead was never more than one second, with the first lap alone seeing four different leaders, while the lap record was smashed repeatedly. After winning the Superstock, his second race victory in one day, Hutchinson commented:

> I can't believe it .... I didn't feel I was on the pace, to begin with, but I got stuck in and had a much better second lap. We filled the tank right up to the brim... at the fuel stop and couldn't get the cap back on. I thought about going off without it, but that would have been stupid![92]

In second place, with an average race speed of 127.349mph, was the 1000cc Honda of Guy Martin, who said, 'Fair play to Ian, there were a few back-markers in the way, on the final lap, he had to deal with them as well, but 129 mph – that's going some.[93]

The machine had been refurbished for the 2010 event, and Clive Padgett's meticulous preparation and attention to detail were certainly factors that contributed to the team's remarkable reliability. While other teams suffered repeated malfunctions and breakdowns, the Padgetts machines remained tightly on the straight and narrow. That year's Royal London 360 Superstock race was to be one of the most thrilling in TT history, and of the five races he won that week, Hutchinson identifies it as his best memory of the 2010 TT. Bear in mind that he had already won a TT (the Supersport race) that same morning, but incredibly went on to make it two wins in just one day, repeating his feat from 2009. In that afternoon's Superstock TT he snatched victory from second-place man Ryan Farquhar by a mere 1.32 seconds, and delivered an astonishing 130.74mph lap on what was to all intents and purposes a standard road bike – the first-ever 130mph lap by a street-legal machine.

Dungannon-man Farquhar, riding a Kawasaki ZX10 he had prepared himself, was aiming for his first TT win since 2005, and knew that the Superstock was his best chance of achieving this. The Irishman put in one of the greatest performances of his career, leading for much of the race, and entered the pits with a lead of 8.8 seconds over Hutchinson, only for a problem with the fuel filler to delay him and cost him dearly. He was not the only one to suffer misfortune, because on the penultimate lap confusion between a marshal (who was signalling for an oil spill at Governor's Dip) and Ian Hutchinson almost caused the latter to pull in, believing that the race had been red-flagged. When Hutchinson realised there was still everything to play for, his blood was up and he was now on a real mission. On the final lap Farquhar still held the lead, but the Bingley man's Honda had greater climbing power and, coming back over the mountain for the last time, and on the descent into Douglas, it was advantage Hutchinson by 1.29 seconds. The end of the race was edge-of-the-seat stuff as the two battled it out over the final furlong, but Hutchy put together an astonishing final lap, beating the old record by 6.61 seconds. Farquhar was understandably crestfallen, but for Hutchinson there was only elation as it took his tally for the week

Ian Hutchinson leans the Padgetts Honda into the bend at Creg-ny-Baa, in the 2010 Superstock TT. (Courtesy of TT Press Office)

to three wins, an astonishing achievement in its own right, which only a handful of other riders have managed. Hutchinson told reporters afterwards of several massive, albeit controlled, slides as he battled his way around the course, adding:

> The Superstock race was a proper close race and a real pleasure to win... I want to win races genuinely and with all the top runners still in the race so people can't say 'Oh he only won because so-and-so broke down'. I don't think the TT has ever been more competitive than it is now. Even when Steve Hislop and Carl Fogarty were racing, it was only those two that were in with a shout, whereas now there's about six guys who could win any particular race. So its good for me to be winning at this time because in years to come people will look back and say it was a really competitive era... The last lap of the Superstock race was the best lap I've ever done round the Isle of Man on any bike... John McGuinness says I've not had enough credit for that and he also said it was the best lap of the whole 2010 TT. It was nearly a 131mph lap on a Superstock bike and no matter what people were saying on the forums about the bike not being legal, I was there watching when Clive Padgett wheeled it out of the showroom as an absolutely standard road bike that was up for sale and he set to work preparing it and just built an awesome bike.[94]

The reliability that characterised the Padgetts bikes in 2010 was purely the product of experience. Clive Padgett, in reflecting on the events of that year, commented:

> We've all been brought up around motorcycles and during a normal week away from the TT we work on everything from 50cc scooters to Honda Goldwings. Our team is so experienced. I'm not being funny here, but if you look in our garage there's not a man under the age of 40! But that's a compliment – it means they're all hugely experienced. Another huge plus point is that all of our team, apart from one man, has actually raced bikes. That's a big thing in understanding the requirements of the bikes we prepare to race and the requirements of our riders.[95]

With two more wins to his name later that week, Hutchinson scaled a summit never before climbed at the TT – a feat which may never be equalled, let alone topped. It became a standing joke that year that the only competitors who were cheerful were the sidecar crews, because theirs was the only class in which Hutchinson was not racing! That year, as often before, at the end

The smiles say it all. Hutchinson and Clive Padgett enjoying the taste of victory at the 2010 TT. (Dave Collister collection/Lily Publications)

of race week the TT organisers took the race winners for a parade of honour along Douglas Promenade in front of crowds of cheering fans. What was different in 2010, however, was the fact that there were only two winners – double TT-winning sidecar driver Klaus Klaffenböck, and Ian Hutchinson. So the Superstocker, which won the event in two separate years, and played a part in one of the most memorable weeks in TT history, finds a place in the top twenty-five TT motorcycles and sidecars. Hutchinson is on record as stating that if the 2010 Superstock machine ever became available he would dearly love to add it to his personal collection, but at the time of writing it remains in Batley, in the hands of TT maestro Clive Padgett.

Chapter 25

BMW S1000RR
(rider Michael Dunlop)
2014

The final machine in our panoply of TT greats is the product of the highest traditions in German automotive engineering, and continues a long and proud history of competition at the TT by BMW. It also stands proudly as part of the tradition of one of the greatest family dynasties to have taken part in racing on the Isle of Man, for machine number twenty-five is that ridden to victory in the 2014 Senior TT by Michael Dunlop, son of Robert Dunlop and nephew of the late great Joey Dunlop.

The German firm's S1000RR motorcycle was designed initially to take part in the 2009 World Superbike championship. It was unveiled in Munich in 2008, and in a speech delivered on 16 April of that year, Hendrick von Kuenheim, the president of the company's motorcycle arm, BMW Motorrad, explained that the new S1000RR was part of an ambitious plan by BMW to increase motorcycle sales by approximately fifty per cent by the year 2012, to 150,000 units. The German marque entered into the superbike realm specifically to take a slice of this Japanese-dominated pie. Citing the eighty-five per cent share of the 1000cc market then held by the big four Far East motorcycle firms, Kuenheim acknowledged the ambitious nature of BMW's superbike project:

> We naturally realise that we are taking on a great challenge. Particularly [as] the Japanese are some 20 years ahead of us in this class and have lots of experience. But even so, the spirit of this competition alone encourages us in our efforts.[96]

The machine they developed is powered by an in-line four-cylinder engine, delivering over 200bhp at 14,000rpm, has 44mm Öhlins forks, and in racing trim it has a wet weight of only 162kg. It made its competitive debut in 2009, with rather modest results in the World Superbike championship, but in 2010 it took the two-wheeled racing world by storm. It utterly dominated every Superstock championship that year, taking the European Superstock title, the British Superstock title and similar honours in France, Spain, Germany, Australia and Canada. In 2010 the machine was brought to the TT by experienced competitor Keith Amor, who was clocked at 189mph on the Sulby Straight. Amor later described the machine as 'an absolute missile,' while in 2011, German development rider Rico Penzkofer brought a semi-official BMW-backed machine to the TT, stating: 'I would say that, currently, the BMW S1000RR is the best Superbike in the world, and I believe that, with the right rider, it is possible to win the TT on it.'[97]

By 2014, that crucial combination of rider and machine had finally come together when Michael Dunlop unexpectedly parted company with Honda. There were reports in the motorcycle press in the early part of the year that Dunlop would be without a ride for the 2014 TT, but at short notice he agreed to ride for Hawk BMW, a team run by Stuart Hicken, who had previously provided motorcycles for his father. Dunlop, whose brother William also races on the Isle of Man, made his Mountain Course debut in 2006 and quickly established a name for himself, both for his skill on the track, and for his uncompromising nature. Dunlop does what he wants to do, for himself, and finds the restrictions of a factory contract confining – hence his frequent shifts between manufacturers and teams. On this occasion, however, he had walked away from a known quantity – the Honda superbike – to something that was completely unproven, the BMW.

BMW Motorrad UK had entered into road-racing in 2014 to celebrate Georg 'Schorsch' Meier's famous Isle of Man victory of seventy-five years previously, in which he rode his factory Type 255 Kompressor and took BMW Motorrad's first ever TT win in the 1939 Senior. Joining forces with Hawk Racing, the team behind the Buildbase BMW Motorrad British Superbike entry, and supported by BMW Motorrad Motorsport, BMW Motorrad/Hawk Racing was formed. The experts from the Munich factory also helped with their expertise, and with additional technical support. For example, BMW Motorrad Motorsport supplied the Superbike engine for Dunlop's RR, which was built to World Superbike specifications using lightweight titanium parts, and was able to produce 222bhp (some 30bhp more than the production model). The bike itself was also set up to withstand the bumpy TT circuit, with all bolts made of steel rather than titanium (also lockwired and silicone sealed), making it somewhat heavier than the short-circuit version at 180kg.

Beginning with the North West 200 in May 2014, Dunlop and the team began to feel their way on it. Although they took victories in both the Superstock and Superbike classes at that meeting, the bike was still far from a finished product, and although it had ample power, Dunlop had to fight with it to retain control. The question now was how would it behave at the next meeting, the Isle of Man TT? Although the BMW Motorrad/Hawk Racing team would add a further three TT trophies to the tally, proving beyond doubt that the BMW S1000RR is a force to be reckoned with in road racing, perhaps only Michael Dunlop could have delivered that result on the bike in its raw state. In the process twenty-five-year-old Dunlop also secured his own place in history, by increasing his total to a stunning eleven TT wins, three of them coming that week onboard BMW S1000RR machines in the Superbike, Superstock and Senior TT races. He also became the first rider in history to win four TT races in two consecutive years.

Thus the machine which takes us to number twenty-five in our tally of all-time great machines is the Superbike version of the S1000RR, winner of both the big races at the 2014 TT, delivering BMW's first superbike win and their first Senior TT victory since 1939. Dunlop had given spectators a hint of what to expect when, in the final practice lap late on Friday night, he almost matched the outright lap record aboard the machine. Only Stuart Hicken, his son Steve who was also team manager, and the Hawk mechanics knew the efforts Dunlop had gone to in order to control it. Then, the following morning, in near perfect conditions in each of the first two laps of the Superbike race, he shattered that record, first with a lap of 131.730mph from a standing start, and next with a lap of 131.890mph. Dunlop, riding as number six, charged through the field in the opening stages and was in the lead by Ballaugh Bridge, a position from which he never wavered. His only real challenger in the race was fans' favourite and TV star Guy Martin, riding for Tyco Suzuki, who admitted afterwards that he was riding as hard as he possibly could to catch Dunlop, and scaring himself repeatedly in the process, but to no avail. The Northern Irishman's only moment of concern came at Ramsey Hairpin on the last lap, where he narrowly avoided colliding with a back marker. Afterwards Dunlop paid tribute to the robustness of the machine, telling *Bike Sport News*:

> For a bike to last around the TT, especially the way I bust 'em, is just fantastic. The BMW is only just showing its potential; there's a lot more to come from that bike. My team were up all night working like dogs sorting my bikes... I can't say enough about the whole team, We have five more races to do this week and three gallons of beer to drink tonight![98]

In reality the poor handling of the machine had been a major problem, but its sheer power output – 215 bhp – and Dunlop's physical ability to handle the bike, had overcome it. Now there was real interest in the machine, and not just from the assembled press. Top executives at BMW flew to the Island to see for themselves what this motorcycle was capable of in the right hands.

However, the handling problems had not gone away, and Senior TT at the end of the week was to prove just as dramatic as the Superbike race. Despite an early challenge from his brother William Dunlop, Michael never really appeared to be under any real threat of losing this most prestigious of the TT races. (So hard was William trying, that he ended up crashing at Graham's, the fast left-hander after the Veranda on the Mountain section and was airlifted to hospital suffering from a suspected broken leg.) Michael took the win by a comfortable fourteen seconds from Isle of Man resident and local hero Conor Cummins on his Honda CBR1000RR Fireblade, with Guy Martin taking third on his Suzuki GSX-R1000. Fourth place went to Bruce Anstey, who seemed to struggle with the blistering early race pace and only started to get into the kind of form that saw him log a 132mph lap record in practice week much too late into the race. Fifth place was taken by James Hillier, ahead of twenty-one-times TT winner John McGuinness, who was struggling with a

Michael Dunlop powers the 1000cc BMW down from the Mountain in the 2014 Senior TT. (Courtesy of TT Press Office)

broken wrist that plagued him all through practice and race week. It was no secret that words had been exchanged between the Dunlop brothers at the earlier North West 200 meeting and the icy atmosphere between them lasted through the 2014 TT, but Michael was visibly concerned for his brother after the race, though he was by then reported as being stable in hospital.

Sealing a win like this was advertising gold dust for the Munich factory, and a short while later official reaction appeared on the BMW Motorrad website. It issued a statement from Michael Dunlop which read:

Every TT win is a great moment, but we did it for BMW, we made history and it will always be remembered. It was just a fantastic feeling to know that they employed me to win races and to repay them after 75 years. For me, that'll always be in the history books. It's been great for me and great for BMW so it was a 'win-win' situation. There were a lot of things going on. The factory hadn't been there in 75 years, the bike itself had never won around there, we hadn't done any testing on the bike – it was too late – so it was good to rock up there with the bike and just do the job straightaway. There was definitely some pressure for everybody involved. I only play a small part in the job. We had engineers there, chassis builders, electronics people. There was a lot of stuff riding on everyone else's shoulders. I just sit on the bike and twist the throttle but they have to make sure everything's right. But the whole package just seemed to work fine. To go with a complete different set-up, with a different bike, with a team that had never been there before, and with no testing – everyone thought we were stupid but we ended up showing them that we were all right. We pulled it off, that was the main thing!

...Then we went to the TT and it was hard work but we made it happen. We did everything we needed to and I just clicked with the bike straightaway and thought 'yes, this is good'.

...The whole weekend, every race that I started, I just upped the pace and then backed off, upped it and backed off again. I rode one fast lap when I really needed to and then just toured the rest, so it really worked well this year.[99]

Udo Mark, BMW Motorrad Motorsport Marketing Director, added some comments from the perspective of the company:

This is a very proud moment for BMW Motorrad Motorsport, there could be no better way to celebrate the 75th anniversary of Schorsch Meier's victory than to return to the Isle of Man and to win again. Congratulations

Michael Dunlop shakes hands with BMW Motorrad Press Manager Lee Nicholls, after the historic 2014 Senior TT win. (Courtesy of TT Press Office)

to Michael and the team. They have shown an unbelievable performance in winning all three races. We are very proud that we played our part and that our joint effort with the team led to this historic triple.[100]

So much for the marketing speak. When Dunlop released his much-anticipated autobiography in 2017 he lifted the lid on what it had really been like to battle with the untamed beast that was the BMW S1000RR, saying of the 2014 Senior TT:

I got the win. I blew everyone away but it wasn't pretty and it wasn't pain-free. When I took my gloves off, blood was pouring out of my hands. My shoulder was knackered. I felt like I'd been chucked out of a window and run over, then chucked out the window again. But we'd done it. Another win, another TT... It took me a while to recover physically. I was lucky I had the strength to make the bike work in the first place. A weaker man would have been thrown off. There were places where she was a bucking bronco, there's no other way of describing it.

In a way, that bike, for all her problems, suited me. I like to tame a bike. When I race, I put the motorbike where I want it to be rather than let it put me where it needs to be. I'm probably one of the few who do that, if not the only one. You watch me race that BMW and it looks like we're in a punch up.[101]

Directly after the Senior win it was announced that the bike would be sent to the BMW museum in Munich, where it would be displayed alongside the 1939 Senior machine of Georg Meier, after a tour of the autumn motorcycle shows. The significance of this fact was not lost on Dunlop, who told reporters that he had never had a bike which he had ridden put in a museum before.

The 2014 factory BMW superbike rounds off the top twenty-five TT Titans in fine style. The significance of the company's achievement that year is hard to overstate. To come to the TT with machines that were to all intents and purposes untested, and to better teams like Honda and Suzuki with their many years of TT experience, was a remarkable accomplishment. They broke Honda's nine-year stranglehold on the Senior TT, and threw down a gauntlet to the other big manufacturers. The reaction in the paddock was almost immediate, and it was noticeable how many other teams – Northern Ireland-based Tyco Racing among them – switched to BMW machinery in the aftermath. As a result the 2020s at the TT promise to be an interesting decade. The old cosy rivalry between Honda, Yamaha, Suzuki and Kawasaki has been blown wide open. And who knows, if the Norton revival continues at the pace it has between 2014 and 2017, we may yet see a return to the 1930s with another big Norton versus BMW showdown. Bring it on!

Epilogue

It would be almost inconceivable to conclude a book such as this without at least some discussion of which of the twenty-five motorcycles and sidecars examined in the preceding pages is – arguably – the overall greatest TT machine of the last 111 years. Inevitably, personal preference will play a large part in any debate along these lines. The age of the reader, the era in which they most often visited the TT, or his or her individual memories of a rider or race will, to a greater or lesser extent, colour the perception of which is the greatest. Further, one might have a bias towards solos or sidecars, or a particular adherence to a manufacturer.

The greatest TT machine of them all? Hailwood in action aboard the Sports Motorcycles Ducati in 1978. (Bikesport Fottofinders archives)

It is also difficult, looking back over eleven decades, to compare machines from different eras fairly. So much has changed in terms of speeds, road conditions and the equipment aboard a motorcycle such as brakes (and more especially engines) that it is rather like trying to compare apples and oranges! Rules have also changed, so that even comparing machines from the same class in different eras is difficult.

Yet in trying to take a purely objective view, it would seem that one machine stands out above all the others, and this is simply because it ticks so many boxes. It was the product of one man's engineering excellence, but its success was also due to another man's riding brilliance. It took part in an epic race, which drew record crowds, bettered the big factory machines, and set new records as it did so. It is associated with perhaps the greatest name ever to appear at the Isle of Man. Above all, it is encapsulated by a story which sums up the against-the-odds spirit of the TT so remarkably well. Not only did its rider achieve what seemed at the time to be impossible, and come back to the Isle of Man after eleven years away and win, but its creator built a machine that took on the might of multinational Honda, and won.

That machine is the 1978 Hailwood Ducati.

Notes

1. *TT Special*, 3 June 1954
2. *TT Special*, 3 June 1954
3. G.S. Davison, *Racing Reminiscences*, Birmingham, 1948, p.69
4. *Ibid*, p124
5. *TT Special*, 3 June 1954
6. *Ramsey Courier*, 4 July 1911
7. John C. Otto, *How Indian Won the Tourist Trophy*, Springfield, Mass., 1911, p.6
8. *TT Special*, 7 June 1948 p.13
9. *TT Special*, 7 June 1948 p.13
10. *TT Special*, 7 June 1948 p.13
11. *Isle of Man Times*, 16 June 1923
12. *Veteran and Vintage Magazine*, May 1960 p.628
13. Quoted in Ruth Cowin, *T.M. Sheard: The Modest Manxman*, Isle of Man, 2006, p.87
14. *Ibid.*, p.87
15. Davison, *Racing Reminiscences*, p.28
16. *Ibid.*, p.64
17. *Ibid.*, p.28
18. Stanley Woods, interviewed by Ivan Rhodes. Ivan Rhodes archive
19. *Ibid.*
20. *Ibid.*
21. *The Motor Cycle*, 29 June 1939
22. *TT Special*, 12 June 1939
23. *The Motor Cycle*, 29 June 1939 p.370
24. *The Motor Cycle*, 29 June 1939 p.370
25. *The Motor Cycle*, 10 April 1947 p.231
26. *Classic Bike*, July 2002, p.23
27. www.motorcycle-klose.blogspot.com/2008/12/rex-mccandless-and-featherbed-frame.html
28. Geoff Duke, *In Pursuit of Perfection*, London, 1988, p.41
29. *Motor Cycling*, 22 June 1950 p.190
30. *Motor Cycling*, 22 June 1950 p.190
31. John Surtees, *Speed*, London 1964, p.94
32. *Ibid.*, p.97
33. Mick Walker, *Bob McIntyre the Flying Scot*, 2006, p.115

34. Stan Hailwood, *The Hailwood Story*, Peterborough, 1966, p.24

35. *Ibid.*, p.25

36. *Daily Mirror*, 23 June 1961

37. www.murraysmotorcycles.weebly.com/history.html

38. *Motorcycle Weekly*, 9 June 1973 p.8

39. *TT Special*, 4 June 1973 p.14

40. www.hbs-bmw.de/

41. Mick Grant, *Taking the Mick*, Yeovil, 2012, p.111

42. Bob Currie, *The Glory of the Manx Tourist Trophy: 1907-1975*, sl, 1976, p.92

43. *TT Special*, 5 June 1974

44. Mick Grant, *Road Racing*, London, 1979, p.109

45. *Motorcyclist Illustrated*, October 1974, p.22

46. *The Motor Cycle*, 7 June 1975 p4

47. Kenny Arthur, interviewed by author

48. George O'Dell and Ian Beacham, *Sidecar Championship*, London, 1978, p.81

49. *Ibid.*, p82

50. Kenny Arthur, interviewed by author

51. *Ibid.*

52. O'Dell and Beacham, *Sidecar Championship*, p.86

53. www.sportsmotorcyclesducati.com

54. www.sportsmotorcyclesducati.com

55. Ted Macauley, *Mike The Bike - Again*, London, 1980, p.52

56. *Ibid.*, p.53

57. Grant, *Takin' the Mick*, p.149

58. Grant, *Roadracing*, p.108

59. *Ibid.*, p.108

60. Macauley, *Mike The Bike - Again*, p.73

61. *Ibid.*, p.73

62. *Motorcycle Sport*, January 1980 p.27

63. Macauley, *Mike the Bike - Again*, p.80

64. *Ibid.*, p.82

65. *Motor Cycle News*, 10 June 1981

66. *Ibid.*,

67. Jack Muldoon. Correspondence with author

68. *Ibid.*

69. *Ibid.*

70. *Ibid.*

71. *Ibid.*

72. *Ibid.*

73. Carl Fogarty, *Foggy: The Explosive Autobiography*, London, 2001 p.157

74. *Ibid.*, p.157

75. *Island Racer*, 2002 p.108

76. Stuart Barker, *David Jefferies - the Official Biography*, Sparkford, 2009, p.209

77. www.davidjefferiesracing.com

78. *Motor Cycle News*, 5 June 2002

79. Barker, *David Jefferies, the Official Biography*, p.223

80. *Motor Cycle News*, 16 June 2004 p58

81. Dave Molyneux, *The Racer's Edge*, Barnsley, 2011 p.96

82. *Ibid.*, p.99

83. *Ibid.*, p.100

84. *Ibid.*, p.102

85. *Motor Cycle News*, 13 June 2007

86. www.motorcyclespecs.co.za

87. *Motor Cycle News*, 13 June 2007

88. www.motorcyclenews.com/sport/2007/june/june0507superstocktt-/

89. www.roadracing world.com

90. www.roadracing world.com

91. www.motorcycle-usa.com

92. www.haltenraum.com

93. www.haltenraum.com

94. Isle of Man TT programme 2011, p.31

95. Isle of Man TT programme 2015, p.133

96. www.motorcycle-usa.com/2008/04/article/2009-bmw-superbike-s1000rr-unveiled/

97. Isle of Man TT programme 2011, p.107

98. *Bike Sport News*, 5 June 2014 p.16

99. www.brand.bmw-motorrad.com/en/stories/speed-world/interview-dunlop-tt-trophy.html

100. www.bmw-motorrad.nl/nl/nl/index.html?content=http://www.bmw-motorrad.nl/nl/nl/fascination/motorsport/index.jsp&id=2949

101. Michael Dunlop, *Road Racer*, London, 2017 p270

Bibliography

Barker, Stuart *David Jefferies - the Official Biography*, Sparkford, 2009

Battersby, Ray *Team Suzuki: A definitive analysis of the factory's roadracing motorcycles* Stillwater, Minn. 2008

Cakebread, Bill *The Matchless Colliers*, Ninfield, 2016

Cathcart, Alan, 'One Tremendous Triple' in *Classic Racer* November/December 2002

Cowin, Ruth *T.M. Sheard: The Modest Manxman*, Isle of Man, 2006

Currie, Bob *The Glory of the Manx Tourist Trophy: 1907–1975*, sl, 1976

Davison, G.S., *Racing Reminiscences: By Riders of the Past and Present*, Birmingham, 1948

Duke, Geoff *In Pursuit of Perfection*, London, 1988

Dunlop, Michael *Road Racer*, London, 2017

Fern, Dave and Burn, Zoe 'Dunlop Powers to Superbike Glory' in *Bikesport News*, 5 June 2014

Fogarty, Carl *Foggy: The Explosive Autobiography*, London, 2001

Grant, Mick *Roadracing*, London, 1979

Grant, Mick *Takin' the Mick*, Yeovil, 2010

Griffith, John *Famous Racing Motorcycles*, London, 1961

Griffith, John *Historic Racing Motorcycles*, London, 1963

Hailwood, Stan *The Hailwood Story: My Son Mike*, Peterborough, 1966

Hutchinson, Ian and Macauley, Ted *Miracle Man*, London, 2016

Macauley, Ted & Hailwood, Mike *Hailwood*, London, 1969

Macauley, Ted *Mike the Bike Again*, London, 1980

Molyneux, Dave *The Racer's Edge*, Barnsley, 2011

O'Dell, George and Beacham, Ian *Sidecar Championship*, London, 1978

Otto, John C. *How Indian Won the Tourist Trophy*, Springfield, Mass., 1911

Surtees, John *Speed*, London, 1964

Walker, Dave 'Hailwood's TT Ducati' in *Motorcycle Mechanics*, June 1978

Walker, Mick *Bob McIntyre the Flying Scot*, Derby, 2006

Index